3rd

Teaching Bilingual Children

Teaching Bilingual Children

edited by Adrian Blackledge

tb

Trentham Books

First published in 1994 by Trentham Books Limited

Trentham Books Limited
Westview House
734 London Road
Oakhill
Stoke-on-Trent
Staffordshire
England ST4 5NP

British Cataloguing in Publication Data
A catalogue record for this book is available from the British Library.

ISBN: 1 85856 014 4

Cover design by Shawn Stipling using images supplied by
'*Alphabets of the World*', Kemble Press.

Designed and typeset by Trentham Print Design Limited, Chester
and printed in Great Britain by Bemrose Shafron Limited, Chester

Contents

The contributors

Martha Allexsaht-Snider is an assistant professor in the department of Elementary Education at the University of Georgia, USA

Adrian Blackledge is Senior Lecturer in English at Westhill College, Birmingham, UK.

David Corson is Professor at the Ontario Institute for Studies in Education, Ontario, Canada.

Chris Davison is Lecturer in TESOL, University of Melbourne, Australia.

Jeanette Harman is currently Head of Nursery at Yew Tree Community Primary School, Birmingham, UK.

Ann Knight taught for many years in primary schools in Birmingham, UK.

Stephen May has taught in New Zealand schools and in universities and colleges of education in both New Zealand and the UK. He is currently in the Sociology Department, University of Bristol, UK.

Jean Mills is Senior Lecturer in Education at Westhill College, Birmingham, UK. She was formerly Deputy Head of the Primary English as a Second Language Unit, Birmingham.Stephen Nyakatawa has taught in Zimbabwe and Birmingham. He is currently with the Curriculum Development and Review, Advisory and Inspection Service, Derbyshire, UK.

Audrey Osler is Lecturer in Education at the University of Birmingham, UK.

Alison Reeves is a drama practitioner and founder member of VOICEBOX Theatre in Education company in Birmingham, UK.

Iram Siraj-Blatchford is Lecturer in Education at the University of Warwick, UK. She has taught in primary and nursery schools and has been a team leader for multilingual support in Berkshire.

Introduction

Children's primary learning medium is their first language. Yet the conventional policy in the education of children whose mother tongue is a minority language is to replace it with that of the majority as soon as possible. In England in particular, schooling is almost entirely conducted in English, regardless of the first language of the children. This is because policy-makers and practitioners have looked on the needs of minority language groups from a remote, if not always unsympathetic perspective. At best there have been liberal, well-meaning 'multicultural' policies which sought to respect and value the range of 'cultures' existing in inner-city schools. At worst governments and schools have ignored the educational needs of bilingual children. Rarely have minority language communities been fully consulted about the education of their children.

This book provides accounts from a range of international contexts of schools changing to provide better opportunities for children who speak minority languages. This is achieved by making full and authentic use of children's languages in the primary curriculum; by bridging the gulf between school culture and home culture; by recognising the invaluable resource of bilingual school staff; and by involving parents and communities in their children's education.

In Chapter 1 *David Corson* argues that an educational system serving a multilingual society but providing only monolingual schooling exercises power unjustly. Such a system tacitly suppresses minority languages without consulting the interests of their speakers. Corson surveys international research which has found that when children are taught in their minority language for a period before transition to schooling in both minority and majority languages, academic progress is much better than in programmes where the children are taught entirely in the majority language. Children from disadvantaged or oppressed minority groups generally profit from bilingual programmes in which their first language plays the major role, because this lays a language foundation which cannot otherwise be guaranteed. Corson finds that mandatory bilingual programmes maintaining the minority language are needed to avoid the routine injustice of widespread and discriminatory school failure. When minority language maintenance is initiated in a community, the members of that community become the experts, and parents participate in the activities of the school. Only a local community can decide what is really necessary.

In Chapter 2 *Stephen May* describes a school context in which children's languages are central in policy development and curriculum planning. At Richmond Road School in Auckland, New Zealand, language policy arose out of close consultation with all groups in the community. On the school site are a Maori language preschool immersion unit, a Samoan language preschool and a Cook Islands language preschool. The school itself offers a range of language-based programmes, including Maori, Samoan and Cook Islands bilingual groups. Parents are welcome to participate in these programmes. The importance of bilingualism permeates the language philosophy of the school. The whole-school language policy recognises and fosters the close relationship between pupils' language, identity and culture.

It is this relationship which informs the account, in Chapter 3, of a multilingual storytelling project in Birmingham, England. Monolingual teachers provided bilingual children with opportunities to bring to the classroom the languages and stories of their cultures. Pakistani, Bangladeshi and Malaysian children told stories in their home languages, drawing on the wealth of narrative of their home cultures. An additive bilingual education policy does not necessarily require teaching through the minority language; in many contexts this is not practicable. A policy and practice which values and gives status to children's language, culture and home learning environment *is* essential if bilingual children are to achieve their potential. The role of the monolingual teacher is to create an environment in which bilingual children are free to choose which lan-

guage to use in a given context. This will only occur when teachers put cultural and linguistic diversity at the heart of the curriculum.

In Chapter 4 *Alison Reeves* describes the development of bilingual and bicultural Theatre-in-Education programmes in England. Theatre-in-Education programmes presented in more than one language enable *all* children to value a range of languages; for bilingual children such programmes provide opportunities for the development of linguistic and cultural self-esteem. The bicultural content of TIE work can also develop cultural awareness and challenge assumptions in all children, while developing the bicultural skills of minority group pupils. TIE is uniquely placed to enable monolingual and bilingual children to enjoy a learning experience on equal terms.

In Chapter 5 *Martha Allexsaht-Snider* provides an account of the development of a Family Literacy Project in Carpinteria, California. This was a successful project for Spanish-speaking families. It developed from the view that literacy activities are socially constructed, and that parents who speak minority languages have many strengths, which are seldom recognised by schools. Much can be achieved when schools reach out to families and enable them to build on their home literacy environment, their oral story culture and their aspirations for their children's learning.

In Chapter 6 *Chris Davison* finds that Australian policies and practices in teaching English to bilingual children are in the forefront of multicultural education world-wide. One of the most significant of these developments is the 'mainstreaming' of ESL provision. ESL students need both an explicit, planned language programme integrated with their general classwork that takes into account their specialised needs, and on-going maintenance and development of their home language, preferably through a bilingual programme.

In Chapter 7 *Ann Knight* asserts that the development of bicultural skills and understanding is crucial to the progress of minority group children. The reinforcement of home culture from the early years can establish children's self-belief, while the development of biculturalism prepares pupils to function with confidence in public culture. For children whose home culture is very different from that of schooling, the demands of playing by the rules are great. When teachers explicitly teach children bicultural skills they are more likely to use education as a means for empowerment.

In Chapter 8 *Stephen Nyakatawa* and *Iram Siraj-Blatchford* suggest that culture, identity, knowledge, experience and language are so closely interwoven that bilingual children's learning can rarely be wholly effective in a monolingual, monocultural environment. If teaching strategies encourage, value and support the use of home language, children are more likely to share their language and culture freely. Bilingual teachers are likely to enhance the learning progress of bilingual children, unhindered by linguistic or cultural misunderstandings. Stephen Nyakatawa and Iram Siraj-Blatchford call for an increase in ethnic minority and bilingual teachers, and more in-service education for monolingual teachers to learn and understand the cultural, linguistic and attitudinal factors which encourage or inhibit bilingual children's linguistic and cognitive development.

The final three chapters arise from this need for bilingual teachers and non-teaching staff in multilingual schools. In Chapter 9 *Jean Mills* finds that when monolingual teachers are working in multilingual classrooms, the support of bilingual classroom assistants is invaluable. Through these assistants bilingual children can gain access to the curriculum in their home language. However, these staff must not be taken for granted; their bilingualism does not necessarily mean that they are linguistic or cultural experts. The effective use of bilingualism in the classroom is a highly skilled matter. Bilingual classroom assistants deserve to receive proper professional development and career opportunities.

In Chapter 10 *Jeanette Harman* argues that in schools serving minority language communities there is a pressing need for a properly trained, accessible interpreting service. Such a service may narrow the gulf between home and school, enabling parents to have access to information about their children's schooling. In training secondary school students as interpreters, primary school teachers became aware of the students' attitudes to race, language and culture. The students regretted the low status of their home languages, which were falling into disuse. Their use of these languages as community interpreters re-established their linguistic confidence and cultural self-esteem, while facilitating parents' access to their children's teachers.

In Chapter 11 *Audrey Osler* examines the work experiences of bilingual teachers in Britain, noting the disadvantages and discrimination which many have encountered, and discussing the impact of market ideologies

on their careers. School managers must ensure that the rich resource of bilingual teachers is not exploited but supported through a genuine equality of opportunity to progress and develop professionally.

In teaching bilingual children we have reached a land of opportunity. Research and good practice in a range of international contexts shows that the way forward lies in the following directions:

- The use and maintenance of children's home language as a primary learning medium in schools

- The development of children's bicultural skills and understanding, enabling them to achieve their potential even when the culture of the school is very different from that of the home

- The recruitment of bilingual teaching and non-teaching school staff, and the provision of professional development and career openings for these staff

- The full involvement of parents and communities in school policy-making and their children's learning.

These strategies will enable bilingual children to learn in an environment which is working towards justice and equality. As learners this is their right. As educators it is our responsibility and our opportunity.

Adrian Blackledge

Chapter 1

Bilingual education policy and social justice

David Corson

Perhaps the most critical policy decision to be made in any school system is the choice of the language that is to be used as the medium of instruction for children. In 1951 a UNESCO 'committee of experts' ruled that 'it is axiomatic that the best medium for teaching a child' is the child's mother tongue (UNESCO, 1953: 11). The committee claimed that this was the case on psychological, sociological and educational grounds. In this paper I examine the justice and accuracy of this claim. I also look at several specific justice-related issues in bilingual education policy. As recently as the early 1980s hard evidence for or against the above UNESCO claim had not appeared. Part of the reason for this was the difficulty of devising true experimental conditions for comparing (minority) mother tongue schooling with schooling for minority mother tongue children conducted in the majority language. Controlling other variables, while excluding the Hawthorne effect and other intruding factors, proved too difficult for any of the many early studies. From the lack of hard evidence many were ready to conclude that minority mother tongue medium instruction might not really be a substantial pedagogical advantage to children (Fasold, 1984).

1

In the absence of this hard evidence, the conventional policy in education for dealing with speakers of minority languages has been to ignore the minority language and to replace it with the language of education. Often educational authorities have gone beyond simply ignoring the minority language, and there are many documented accounts of injustices regularly inflicted on linguistic minorities in an attempt to eradicate their languages through schooling. Many of these accounts are quite recent and they make harrowing reading (Skutnabb-Kangas, 1981, Baker, 1988, Skutnabb-Kangas and Cummins, 1988, Romaine, 1989). Contemporary school policy makers could claim that these injustices of the past no longer have any currency. However, when a language spoken by a minority is not used in schooling, either as a means of instruction or as a curriculum subject, then it is clear to all concerned that that language is not valued in the school. Moreover if everything that is valued in schooling can be linked to the dominant language and if this linkage is legitimated in the discourses of power that operate in the school, then those past unjust policies of eradication continue in a tacit but recognisable form.

My concern in this paper is to recommend directions that policy makers in education ought to take either to eliminate these continuing injustices or at least to soften their effects. I will argue that an educational system serving a multilingual society but providing only monolingual schooling exercises power unjustly. It is true that the degree of that injustice will vary in line with the Kantian principle that 'ought implies can' : that is to say, schools cannot be held to account for their actions or inactions if they lack the power to act in any other way. But this is only a technical defence for schools themselves and it cannot be used to defend the inactivity of those who do have power to change things. In urging the latter to take policy action that redresses injustice, there are three broad social justice components that are missing from a monolingual system of schooling serving a multilingual society (Corson, 1993). First, following Bourdieu, the schools in that system unjustly require all children to possess the dominant language as cultural capital but fail to guarantee that children *can* acquire that language to an equal degree. Second, following Habermas, the system makes no compromise in respect of the acquired cultural group interest that the minority language represents. In any discussion of social justice and language, considerable room must be left for a collectivist account that gives prominence to the justice needs of social groups,

2

alongside the needs of individuals. Indeed the essential functions of language are to allow and to promote interaction between social groups of two or more people; language has no real existence outside social groups. So in order to support the individual's language, the group's language must be supported at the same time. Finally, following Bhaskar (1989, Corson, 1991a), an unwanted form of determination is at work in the system since it participates in tacitly suppressing a minority language without consulting the interests of its speakers. This unwanted policy needs to be replaced by the wanted form of determination that a just language policy would offer.

Social justice issues in bilingual education

There are so many unresolved issues in contemporary bilingual education that there is a problem separating social justice issues from other more general questions that schools might reasonably attend to in pursuing general educational effectiveness. The basic social justice problem in the education of minorities is to decide where and when we should provide a form of language learning and development that will protect the life chances of children who would otherwise have limited access to social contexts where their mother tongue is used. For those children opportunities to master varieties, styles, registers and functions of their mother tongue may be too few to allow them to function as fully competent speakers of their first language. Consequently, as outlined below, the same children will be placed at risk in learning and using the majority language and in their cognitive/academic activities generally. Much of what follows attends to aspects of this basic problem.

Policies of transitional or maintenance bilingual education?

The bilingual education policy issue is complicated by sharp differences in the value placed on minority languages in the schooling process. The middle stages in the development of minority language policies see the minority language having mainly an instrumental value in learning the majority language; later stages see it having an intrinsic value as well. According to Lambert (1975) the aims of schooling in relation to bilingualism fall into two distinct categories: 'additive bilingualism', when a

3

second language is acquired with the expectation that the mother tongue will continue to be used; and 'subtractive bilingualism', when a second language is learned with the expectation that it will replace the mother tongue (i.e., the minority language) The former is a 'maintenance' form of bilingual schooling which sets out to use both languages as media of instruction for a reasonable amount of the child's school career The latter is a 'transitional' form of bilingual schooling which lasts only for the early years of schooling, with the majority tongue taking over as the means of instruction after that.

Between these two positions an important social justice issue is at stake, hinted at by Horvath (1980) when she says that the US Office of Civil Rights supports the maintenance approach (which is consistent with seeing cultural groups forming a broad mosaic across the nation) while the US Office of Education supports the transitional approach (which is consistent with seeing cultural groups eventually shedding their identity in the melting pot of the American nation). No doubt there are major financial considerations that inform the Office of Education's view. However for reasons of both pedagogy and justice, subtractive (transitional) bilingualism is not a policy that should be routinely favoured in contemporary schools in pluralist societies.

The curriculum evidence

There is much evidence from studies of programmes where majority language speakers have been taught using a minority language as the medium of instruction, but this is not relevant to the subject of this paper: the bilingual education of minorities. Studies of bilingual schooling for majority language speakers, such as the Schools Council Bilingual Education Project in Wales and the St Lambert Project in Canada, are outside my scope here since the provision of bilingual schooling to first-language speakers of a dominant language is not as high a priority on social justice grounds as the provision of bilingual schooling to minorities. Those in immersion programmes for children from majority language backgrounds usually live in communities where the idea of their contact with second-language immersion curricula is supported or at least tolerated. Parental approval of the programmes and their keen support of the children's development in both languages is an accepted part of the arrangements that schools make. So while this evidence offers very positive support to bilingual immersion policies, it is not really helpful here.

Maintenance bilingual programmes for minority language children have been extensively studied in recent years and the evidence comes from many places. In Holland a bilingual maintenance approach to the education of minority children is favoured not just for reasons of social justice and self-esteem, but because it is found to be as effective in promoting majority language learning as other assimilation and transition approaches and even requires less time to be devoted to the teaching and learning of the majority tongue. Other programmes in Leiden and En-schede for the primary age children of Turkish and Moroccan immigrant workers suggest that minority language teaching for children from these backgrounds has no negative educational or social effects (Appel, 1988). In short these Dutch maintenance programmes achieve only good results. Moorfield (1987) reviews programmes over the last twenty years in Mexico, the USA, Sweden and Canada where children began school speaking a minority language or dialect and where that language was used as the main or only medium of instruction. Later, for all these children there was a gradual transition to instruction in both the minority and the majority language. Academic progress achieved in each case was much better than in programmes where minority language children were taught entirely in the majority language. Student self-esteem, pride in their cultural background and group solidarity also increased in each case. In other settings, where the needs for bilingualism and biliteracy are so obvious that the question of desirability is never even raised, initial and advanced literacy in two languages becomes possible and full bilingual-ism becomes a natural and necessary acquisition for all children (Garcia and Otheguy, 1987).

In the USA, a long-term comparison study examined three approaches to bilingual schooling for Hispanic children (Chamot, 1988):

1. immersion strategy, in which content subjects are taught through simplified English;

2. early-exit or short-term transitional bilingual programmes of two to three years;

3. late-exit or long-term transitional bilingual programmes of five to six years.

Researchers found that long-term bilingual curriculum programmes are most effective in promoting progress in both Spanish and English and that immersion programmes promote a greater use of English by students in school itself. Elsewhere in the USA, Spanish-dominant children attending schools in California benefited both academically and in their English language acquisition by having their mother tongue used as the language of instruction in the early junior school years (Campos and Keatinge, 1988).

In Sweden a policy of 'active bilingualism' has been the goal for immigrant pupils' language learning since 1975 and it has been a legal right since 1977. The official Swedish policy of 'freedom of choice' extended to its immigrants in their decisions about maintaining their own cultures and languages is consistent with the justice criteria derived from Bhaskar, Bourdieu and Habermas. It means in practice that every immigrant child, from any minority group which is large enough, must have the opportunity to attend a mother-tongue-medium class. Classes for the large Finnish minority in suburban Stockholm, segregated into classes using Finnish as the medium of instruction with Swedish taught as a second language, are among the longest established (Hagman and Lahdenpera, 1988). After nine years of operation researchers base their conclusions on extensive comparisons with other Finnish children and with other immigrant groups who have not had a rich history of instruction in their mother tongues. By the end of their compulsory schooling the segregated Finnish maintenance children have still managed to integrate themselves into their Swedish comprehensive school while building up their academic self-confidence, identity and their proficiency in Swedish. Moreover the students from the Finnish maintenance classes show much higher figures for entry into further education.

In Britain the MOTET project in Bradford (Fitzpatrick, 1987) assessed the effects of bilingual education in a one-year experimental programme with infant children whose home language was Panjabi. The class programme aimed to preserve a 'parity of esteem' between English and Panjabi by allotting equal time and space to each language across the curriculum. The study concluded that there were no negative effects from bilingual education. Instead there were positive effects of mother tongue maintenance as well as a level of progress in English that was equivalent to a matched control group who had not received a bilingual programme.

Finally the special needs of the French Canadian population provide a spur to research and changes in practice in Canada, where more than 288,000 children were in French immersion classes in 1990 and 58% of the population endorsed the 'two official languages' policy. Francophone minority children in Ontario schools who receive most of their education in French tend to succeed much better in education and in the world of work than those submerged in English or in only nominally bilingual schools (Churchill et al., 1986). Cummins and Swain (1986) provide a general guide to the research in bilingual education taking place in Canada. The authors overturn many of the prejudiced views that have been widely held about bilingualism and education:

● they show that the research base for bilingual education is sophisticated and growing

● they offer strong evidence that quality bilingual programmes have been influential in developing language skills and in contributing to broader academic achievement

● they deny the conventional view that immersion programmes can only be effective with the very young

● they suggest that in some respects older learners have advantages over younger ones

● they report evidence that lower ability children also benefit from immersion programmes;

● they conclude that a quality bilingual programme will support and aid development in the first language.

This international survey of curriculum research and the conclusions that follow from it raise difficult issues that have profound justice implications for language policy making. In the following sections I try to present and resolve those issues.

How much first language maintenance is needed?

Following ideas first expressed by Finnish researchers Toukamaa and Skutnabb-Kangas, Cummins and Swain (1986) put forward a 'threshold hypothethis': there may be threshold levels of language competence which bilingual children must attain in their first and second languages in

7

order to avoid cognitive disadvantages and to allow the potentially beneficial aspects of becoming bilingual to influence cognitive functioning.
While the researchers cannot define threshold levels in absolute terms,
since these will vary as the cognitive levels of children and the academic
demands of the school vary, this hypothesis explains many different
phenomena. At the same time it still needs strong empirical support,
especially at the level of language itself. Cummins, for example, assumes
that language proficiency is an important mediating variable between
bilingualism and education, but he is criticised by some for not saying
much about the specific linguistic advantages that being bilingual brings:
the preconditions for literacy in speech, as distinct from the more obvious
educational advantages that are spelled out by him rather vaguely as
'literacy related skills'.

In her critique of the threshold hypothesis, Romaine (1989) warns
against compartmentalising of language skills removed from other knowl-
edge-related factors. I believe that research has not yet broached the major
epistemic questions about the two cultural worlds to which bilinguals have
access and the effect of this access on their linguistic and intellectual
development. It may turn out that young bilingual children bring intellectual skills to school that are not recognised or used in the curriculum only
because the present excessively structured and normative view of child
development insists that the onset of those sophisticated skills occurs
much later in childhood and even in adulthood.

Cummins and Swain do provide evidence to show that there are aspects
of language proficiency that are common to both first and second languages; aspects that are interdependent/This evidence suggests why less
instruction in the second language often results in higher second-language
proficiency scores for minority students, while for majority language
students more instruction in the second language results in higher second-
language proficiency scores. They also argue that in some aspects of
second-language learning older learners are more efficient learners and
they offer guidance to curriculum policy-makers interested in producing
bilingual proficiency.

Three key points about bilingualism and schooling follow from their
discussion:

● a high level of proficiency in both languages is likely to be an intellectual advantage to children in all subjects across the curriculum, when compared with their monolingual classmates

● in social situations where there is likely to be serious erosion of the first (minority) language, that language needs development and maintenance if intellectual performance is not to suffer

● high-level second-language proficiency depends on welldeveloped first-language proficiency.

From these three points it seems that children from disadvantaged or oppressed minority groups generally profit from bilingual programmes in which their first language plays the major role, because this lays a language foundation which cannot otherwise be guaranteed. This conclusion contrasts with the findings for children from dominant majority language groups who benefit from bilingual programmes in which the second language is used more frequently (Appel and Muysken, 1987). In the latter case a firm foundation in the first language occurs naturally because it is the language of wider communication in the society.

The third point above, that learning a second language well depends on developing prior proficiency in the first, is broadly consistent with the findings of educators in the USSR whose experience in these matters outstrips experiences elsewhere (McLaughlin, 1986). Also, research in Germany strongly links high-level development in conceptual information and discourse strategies in the first language with high-level second-language development (Rehbein, 1984). From all this research comes a general conclusion about schooling up to the present that seems to have great explanatory power; for more than a century of compulsory schooling in English-speaking countries, the stress on teaching only English as a second language to young minority language speakers early in their schooling has been a misplaced emphasis that has probably brought tragic consequences to many of the recipients of that schooling. In many educational systems the tragedy continues.

There seems to be relevance in all this for the education of large minority language groups in the countries of North America, Australasia, Britain and Southern Africa. First, because their languages are not the languages of wider communication, ancestral minority language-speaking children whose languages and cultures have been marginalized by

9

invasion cultures may arrive in schools with their first languages relatively under-developed in certain contexts, styles and function of use. At the same time their grasp of the majority language may be limited to a relatively small range of functions often related to passive activities such as television viewing and the like. Second, because there may be only occasional use of their first languages outside the home, children from some minority settler backgrounds may similarly arrive in school with their first languages relatively under-developed in certain school-linked ways and with less than optimum development in the majority language. For all these children intensive early exposure in school to the majority language, accompanied by school neglect of their first language, may result in low achievement in the majority language as well as a decline in mother-tongue proficiency. The recommendation for policy makers seems a straightforward one: mandatory bilingual programmes maintaining the minority language are needed to avoid the routine injustice of widespread and discriminatory school failure.

Research on the best age for introducing the majority or dominant language

Very young children (under five), given a suitable environment such as that offered by Maori 'language nests' in New Zealand or French immersion pre-schools in Canada, acquire a second language quickly and seem to pick up two languages simultaneously without much difficulty. Although most theorists agree that there is some advantage in a very early start in second-language learning, the causes and the nature of that advantage are far from clear. The situation becomes more complex for older children.

Swedish research (Skutnabb-Kangas, 1981) found that Finnish children moving to Sweden and learning Swedish early in their school careers lost much of their proficiency in Finnish. Others who moved later (at ten years) maintained a level of Finnish very close to their age mates in Finland while also acquiring proficiency in Swedish. Even allowing, as Harley (1986) suggests, that different social influences could have influenced the younger children's academic performance, arriving as they did so young in a new culture where they were negatively stereotyped, it is the case that similarly adverse social factors often affect young language learners in a new culture. I believe that the age-related results of the

10

Swedish study are significant whether we explain them in purely linguistic or in sociocultural terms as well. Support for this view comes from Canadian studies of immigrant Japanese children; there is evidence from Holland and Indo-China too that older children manage to maintain and develop cognitive and academic skills in their first language to a greater extent than younger immigrant children (Cummins et al., 1984) and children between nine and twelve years also make more rapid progress in academic aspects of their second language than do children between five and eight years (Appel and Muysken, 1987).

Two points stand out in the above which allow firm policy conclusions. First, it seems very important that the minority child's first language is given maximum attention up to the stage of middle schooling so that skill in using it to manipulate abstractions develops and so that it can be used to perform the cognitive operations necessary for acquiring the second language. This is not happening in many places; in most public school systems in the USA, in Australasia and in Britain. Nor is it happening in very different places like Hong Kong, where English-medium schools in an overwhelmingly Cantonese-speaking city seem to hinder many Cantonese mother tongue students' educational attainment (Yu and Atkinson, 1988). Second, in learning the majority language as a second language, older students, up to the age of early adolescence at least, seem to have a cognitive advantage in performing academic tasks that are context re-duced (e.g., abstract and difficult) (Harley, 1986). Combining these two conclusions, there seems a strong case for deferring formal bilingual programmes until quite late in schooling and concentrating instead on first (minority) language development. In all of the English-speaking countries mentioned above, ESL programmes could come later since the majority language is widely available and constantly reinforced outside the school. In other places like Hong Kong, a curriculum which introduces English gradually as a second language and then uses both languages equally as media of instruction seems warranted so that first-language competence can be supported and used in learning the second. Certainly in each type of setting, the value of beginning formal ESL education should not be considered as a separate policy issue from the learner's first language development.

Difficulties for minority students in transitional classrooms and maintenance classrooms

When transitional programmes address the curriculum through the medium of the majority language even quite proficient bilingual students have difficulties. Skutnabb-Kangas (1981) details these unusual stresses which may be little appreciated by policy makers who have never had to learn another language; listening to a foreign language is more tiring; it requires more intensive concentration; there are fewer redundant sections in discourse so there are fewer opportunities to relax; and when speaking in the second language there is constant pressure to think about the form of language used, allowing less attention to be paid to the content of utterances. Less proficient second-language students, attempting the doubly complex task of taking information from the lesson and learning the language at the same time, are under even greater stress. There is less comprehensible input and less information in general than other students receive; the longer sequences of discourse may be unintelligible because key words are missed; opportunities to relax are fewer but they are more necessary; and the main defence against losing self-confidence may be to switch off from time to time and consciously opt out.

In contrast, in a maintenance bilingual setting, the children can choose when to use the second language; they are motivated to use it whenever they wish rather than expected to use it constantly; and they can resort to the first language whenever it is necessary for clarification, for elaboration or simply just for a break. Says Skutnabb-Kangas:

> All this means, then, that instruction through the medium of L2 during the risk period... does not give the minority child the same possibilities which the native child in the same class has to develop her cognitive/academic language proficiency... and this seems to a certain extent to explain why even extensive exposure to L2 does not necessarily lead to a corresponding development of L2. If the child instead uses the L1 channel for cognitively demanding tasks until the L2 channel is well developed, the common underlying proficiency thus developed also benefits L2 later. (1981: 120).

Baetens Beardsmore (1986) offers other reasons to support a maintenance approach that have a strong linguistic component: in maintenance bilingual programmes teachers are bilingual themselves, even though they may use only one language, and they act positively towards both cultures in the environment. In transitional programmes the teachers are usually monolingual and are often unwittingly hostile to the bilingual element in the child's make-up.

Conclusion

Some high immigrant regions and countries have severe difficulties in providing universal mother tongue maintenance schooling for their highly dispersed but often small groups who speak a diversity of languages. Fasold (1984) suggests some policy criteria to use in deciding on a second language of instruction in those settings where minority bilingual schooling is possible in at least some community languages:

1. where the language is used as a medium of wider communication, among sub-groups who do not share mother tongues, it should be preferred over languages that are not

2. .. where the language has a large number of native speakers (at least 10% of the population) it should be preferred over small-group languages

3. where the language is equipped to serve as a school language, without extensive language engineering, standardisation, specialist teacher training or creation of a literary tradition, it should be preferred over those languages that need a large development effort

4. where minority group preference itself is against the use of their language for educational purposes then this is a strong factor against doing so

5. where members of the minority are dropping out of school in larger numbers than the majority group, this is an important sign that the minority language needs support through its use as a medium of instruction.

Even these very reasonable suggestions from Fasold run into rather straightforward justice issues that cannot be resolved effectively at system level. Policy 2 discriminates against the children of small ethnolinguistic groups who may already be highly discriminated against because their languages are regarded as low in status; policy 3 discriminates against those who may already be highly discriminated against because their culture and language is regarded as low in status; and the UNESCO committee (1953) proposes that ethnic groups of the kind mentioned in policy 4 may need to be educated in the advantages that they are over-looking.

Clearly most decisions about minority languages in pluralist societies need to be made and implemented at the level of the school. Indeed devolving decision making in this way, in any act of social policy, seems a consistent use of the discourse ethic that Habermas has developed (Corson, 1993). On his account, to apply the discourse ethic in policy action does not require a conception of what *the* just society would be. Rather it requires as many conceptions of justice as there are distinct possible conditions of society or subsets of society or culture. Every situation is a new setting for instigating the search for a contextually appropriate conception of justice through the discourse ethic. This being so, it also seems to follow from Habermas that local minority communities should be involved in deciding the shape and direction of their children's schools.

What is becoming clearer, on the evidence from those countries where additive bilingual education for minority peoples is gaining respect, is that the community of minority tongue users themselves can begin to rise in esteem and in political influence at the same time as the rebirth or strengthening of their language. This is a complex phenomenon and there is no simple cause-and-effect relationship between on the one hand increasing levels of bilingualism and on the other an increased social standing for the minority language's users. But where the minority language itself becomes more in charge of the schooling process, the entire programme of schooling is directed towards elevating the status of the community and questioning the role of schooling in that process. Language questions become subsumed under much more important issues, among which language is only an all-pervading and sometimes distracting factor (Garcia and Otheguy, 1987). When minority language maintenance is initiated in a community, the minority members of that community become the experts. They are the advisers and real controllers of the bilingual education programme; their values shape the educational outcomes. Political mobilisation with real purpose can begin to occur. Community attitudes are laid bare and discussed. Local people receive formal training as teachers. Parents participate in the activities of the school to a greater degree and they acquire skills that were previously not their own. All of these things and many more contribute to the elevation of the minority group. Political consciousness awakens where previously there was perhaps none. And the language of the minority becomes available as a recognised political voice at the same time as their political will begins to assert itself.

It is likely that schools controlled and run by remote bureaucracies and staffed by teachers whose culture is not the culture of the local community get in the way of all this. When majority culture educators look at minority children they tend to focus on what those children lack and usually what they see is the absence of a high-level proficiency in the majority language. This lack becomes the focus of the schooling that they offer those children. It is a commonplace for observers of educational reform to claim that policies of compensatory, multicultural and anti-racist education, imposed from afar, make little difference to educational inequality. These policies ignore the root causes of that inequality which is very often linked to an absence of bilingual provision within the curriculum of specific schools. Sometimes that bilingual provision can be aimed at mother tongue maintenance, sometimes at enhancing the cultural esteem of minority groups, sometimes at some combination of these aims. Only a local community can really decide what is necessary. When communities themselves are in charge of education, when they themselves have the respect and the dignity that goes with deciding the future of their offspring, they themselves come to see education in a much broader way. They begin to ask each other about the best way to educate their children and about what is wrong with the alternative processes of schooling that they are familiar with.

This chapter raises many of the social justice issues that are part of the bilingual education policy debate. For a fuller treatment, including a report on the success of various countries in addressing the language needs of minorities, a discussion of the effects of racist ideologies on bilingual policies, and suggestions about what kinds of school action follow from the evidence, see Corson (1993).

References

Appel, R. (1988) 'The language education of immigrant workers' children in The Netherlands', in Skutnabb-Kangas, T. and Cummins, J (eds.) *Minority Education: From Shame to Struggle* (Clevedon, Avon: Multilingual Matters).

Appel, R. and Muysken, P. (1987) *Language Contact and Bilingualism* (London: Edward Arnold).

Baetens Beardsmore, H.(1986) *Bilingualism: Basic Principles* (Clevedon, Avon: Multilingual Matters).

Baker, C. (1988) *Key Issues in Bilingualism and Bilingual Education* (Clevedon, Avon: Multilingual Matters).

Campos, S. and Keatinge, H. (1988) 'The Carpinteria language minority student experience: from theory, to practice, to success', in Skutnabb-Kangas and Cummins, op. cit. pp. 299-307.

Chamot, A. (1988) Bilingualism in education and bilingual education: the state of the art in the United States', *Journal of Multilingual and Multicultural Development*, 9, pp. 11-35.

ChurchilL, S., Frenette, N. and Quazi, S. (1986) *Education et Besoins des Franco-Ontariens: Le diagnostic d'un Systeme d'Education* (Toronto: Le Conseil de l'Education Franco-Ontarienne).

Corson, D. (1991) 'Bhaskar's critical realism and educational knowledge', *British Journal of Sociology of Education*, 12, pp. 223-241.

Corson, D. (1993)*Language, Minority Education and Gender: Linking Social Justice and Power.* Multilingual Matters/OISE Press: Clevedon, Avon.

Cummins, J., Swain, M., Nakajima, K., Handscombe, J., Green, D. and Tran, C. (1984) 'Linguistic interdependence among Japanese and Vietnamese immigrant students', in Rivera, C. (ed.) *Communicative Competence Approaches to Language Proficiency Assessment* (Clevedon, Avon: Multilingual Matters).

Cummins, J. and Swain, M. (1986) *Bilingualism in Education: Aspects of Theory, Research and Practice* (London, Longman).

Fasold, R. (1984) *The Sociolinguistics of Society* (Oxford: Basil Blackwell).

Fitzpatrick, F. (1987) *The Open Door* (Clevedon, Avon: Multilingual Matters)

Garcia, O. and Otheguy, R. (1987) 'The bilingual education of Cuban-American children in Dade County's ethnic schools', *Language and Education: An International Journal*, 1, pp. 83-95.

Hagman, T. and Lahdenpera, J. (1988) 'Nine years of Finnish- medium education in Sweden: what happens afterwards? The education of minority children in Botkyrka', in Skutnabb-Kangas and Cummins, op. cit.

Harley, B. (1986)*Age in Second Language Acquisition* (Clevedon, Avon: Multilingual Matters).

Horvath, B. (1980) *The Education of Migrant Children: A Language Planning Perspective* ERDC Report No 24 (Canberra: AGPS).

Lambert, W. (1975) 'Culture and language as factors in learning and education', in A. Wolfgang (Ed.) *Education of Immigrant Students: Issues and Answers* (Toronto: Ontario Institute for Studies in Education).

Mclaughlin, B. (1986) 'Multilingual Education: theory east and west' in Spolsky, B. *Language and Education in Multilingual Settings* (Clevedon, Avon: Multilingual Matters)

Moorfield, J. (1987) 'Implications for schools of research findings in bilingual education' in Hirsch, W. (ed.) *Living Languages* (Auckland: Heinemann)

Rehbein, J. (1984) *Diskurs und Verstehen: Zur Role der Muttersprache bei der Texverarbeitung in der Zweitsprache* (Hamburg: University of Hamburg)

Romaine, S. (1989) *Bilingualism* (Oxford: Basil Blackwell)

Skutnabb-Kangas, T. (1981) *Bilingualism or Not: The Education of Minorities* (Clevedon, Avon: Multilingual Matters)

Skutnabb-Kangas, T. and Cummins, J. (1988) *Minority Education: From Shame to Struggle* (Clevedon, Avon: Multilingual Matters)

UNESCO (1953) *The Use of Vernacular Languages in Education* (Paris: UNESCO)

Yu, V. and Atkinson, P. (1988) 'An investigation of the language difficulties experienced by Hong Kong secondary school students in English-medium schools', *Journal of Multilingual and Multicultural Development*, 9, pp 267-284.

Chapter 2

School-based language policy reform: a New Zealand example[1]

Stephen May

Much has been written recently on the potential benefits for ethnic minority children of implementing 'language policies across the curriculum' (LPACs) at school level (see, for example, Corson, 1990; Marland, 1977; Maybin, 1985). These theorists have argued for language policies which recognise and incorporate the home languages of minority children within the curriculum. They suggest that inclusive school-based language policies are crucial to empowering minority children whose languages and cultures have been, until now, marginalised in the educational process. Putting this into practice, however, is easier said than done.

As with many previously heralded innovations, there is a noticeable discrepancy between the enthusiastic endorsement of LPACs in the literature and their successful implementation in schools. Many schools are ambivalent about LPACs and/or implement them to little effect. It is argued here that if this is to change, schools need to recognise the organisational, pedagogical and relational demands that the development

1. This chapter is a revised version of an article which first appeared in *Language, Culture and Curriculum* 4, 3, 201-217 (1991). Its inclusion here, in revised form, is by kind permission of Multilingual Matters.

of an LPAC at school level entails. These demands are not insignificant but Richmond Road School in Auckland, New Zealand will be discussed as an example of what can be achieved when these considerations are taken into account. A written policy of the school is also included as a possible model for school-based language policy development.

The Gap Between Theory and Practice

Implementing an LPAC at school level is beset with difficulties. The reasons for this most often centre on a lack of agreement in schools over the aims and scope of an LPAC; an inability to involve all teachers in the development of an LPAC, thus ensuring their support for the policy; and an inability to change school structures to match the inclusive intentions with which LPACs have been largely associated. What results, as has been the case with many other educational innovations, is an enthusiastic endorsement in the literature and an ambivalent and desultory pattern of implementation among practitioners. This is well illustrated by David Corson's observation that such policies 'are viewed by a growing number of educationists as an integral and necessary part of the administrative and curriculum practices of modern schools, yet relatively few schools anywhere have seriously tackled the problem of introducing them' (1990: 1). Achieving a school-based language policy which is inclusive and empowering of minority children is, it seems, no easy task.

If LPACs are to avoid being just another failed educational innovation, the ambiguities surrounding their structure and purposes, and the resulting problems which schools face in their practical implementation, need to be addressed and clarified. In this regard, it is necessary to recognise the difficulties which inhere in any attempt to establish school-based curriculum development (see Skilbeck, 1984; Stenhouse, 1975). As Skilbeck observes, if the school is to establish and implement school-based curriculum development (such as an LPAC) it needs:

> to take bolder initiatives to equip itself as a centre of educational development; to restructure; to build itself into the educational system, not stand apart; and to achieve and demonstrate a practical capability for directing and organising curriculum change. (1984: 207)

Skilbeck goes on to suggest that 'in taking these actions, it is less the independence and self-reliance of the school that need to be fostered than its readiness and ability, as an organisation and a community, to think and act relationally' (*ibid*: 278). What follows is an account of Richmond Road School and its development, over a number of years, of an holistic and inclusive language policy for its predominantly bilingual and ethnic minority pupils. It is my argument that Richmond Road provides us with an example of what can be achieved by a school when it is able 'to think and act relationally' in the way that Skilbeck describes. The resulting school-based language policy, with its effective linking of theory and practice, is a model to which other schools can aspire.

Developing a Whole-School Language Policy

Richmond Road has implemented an LPAC which arises out of the language needs of the school. It is cross-curricular in its concerns, breaking down traditional subject boundaries, and has involved (and continues to involve) the whole school community in its development and implementation. Richmond Road's aim in implementing an LPAC has been to find and agree on the solutions necessary for addressing the language needs of the school. In practical terms, this has led the school to adopt a consultative and collaborative approach to decision-making among its staff, and between the school and its local community. Having identified salient language issues through this consultative process, the school has developed a language policy which sets out what the school intends to do about these areas of concern, provides staff with direction within a discretionary and flexible framework, and provides a statement of action that includes provision for follow up, monitoring and revision in the light of changing circumstances (Corson, 1990). The term 'whole-school policy' (Marland, 1977) describes Richmond Road's language policy well. Marland has argued that whole-school policies analyse the skills and knowledge required in a particular curriculum field, endeavour to establish how these can best be acquired and developed, and plan contexts and activities to provide the best opportunities for practice and use. It is clear, given this definition, that not all LPACs presently operating in schools can be called whole-school policies. The processes attendant on such policies have consequently not been followed, or have only been followed in part, and this may well explain why so many schools have encountered difficulties in effectively implementing LPACs. In contrast, the well established staff development process at Richmond Road, and the coherent educational philosophy which permeates the school, lead to an approach to language, consistent with Marland's observation, which is carried out by teachers 'in the activity context when teaching occurs at the precise point of need, according to the policy, and drawing on the shared knowledge' (1977: 12).

Richmond Road: The Background

The educational approach of Richmond Road School has been discussed in recent literature (see Cazden, 1989; May, 1991; 1993; 1994) but the characteristics of the school are briefly outlined here. The following information about Richmond Road has been gathered over the course of the 1990-1992 school years from interviews and informal discussions with the newly appointed principal and with numerous other staff members on the structure and operation of the school. The extensive documentation the school has itself collected and chronicled on its educational approach has also been drawn upon in the following account.

Richmond Road School is situated in the inner city area of New Zealand's largest city, Auckland. It is a multi-ethnic state primary (elementary) school with approximately 200 pupils and 18 (full-time and part-time) teaching staff. Most of the pupils at the school represent non-dominant groups in New Zealand society, principally of Maori (the indigenous people of New Zealand) and Pacific Island origin. The school's ethnic composition, as of March 1993, comprised: 17% Maori; 15% Pakeha (New Zealanders of European origin); 22% Samoan; 18% Cook Island; 9% Tongan; 9% Niuean. Other significant ethnic groups include: 5% Indian; 4% Chinese. There is a similarly multi-ethnic staff, including representatives of most of the cultural groups to which the majority of pupils belong.

The school draws its pupils from a range of local English and minority language-speaking preschools. On site are a Kohanga Reo (a Maori language preschool immersion unit; literally, 'language nest') that has been operating since 1985: an A'oga Fa'a Samoa (Samoan language preschool) that started in 1989; and Te Apii Reo Kuki Airani (Cook Islands language preschool) that started in 1990. These preschool units aim to foster their respective minority languages through full immersion teach-

22

ing and are part of the recent emergence in New Zealand of such programmes. Other English-speaking preschool units in the area also contribute to the school's clientele.

The school itself offers a range of language-based programmes. In addition to two English-language programmes, there are Maori, Samoan, and Cook Islands bilingual programmes operating within the school. An inner city second language unit also caters for recent arrivals to New Zealand and teaches English, where possible, through the home languages of its students. All these programmes are arranged in vertical *ropu* (the Maori term for group(s)) which are based on the whanau (extended family) model. Each ropu consists of the entire range of pupils from new entrants through to Form 2 (5-13 years old) and children stay in the same ropu, with the same teachers, right through their primary schooling. Parents, on bringing their children to the school, are given the choice of which ropu they wish their children to enter. This overcomes the significant problem of ambivalence or confusion for parents as to the role of home languages in the school (Corson, 1990). Parents are able to clearly identify what the school offers in comparison to others and can then make their choice within the variety of language structures the school itself offers. Teachers have the same pupils for eight years and this means that staff come to know the families particularly well, further fostering community and school interchange over this time.

The vertical ropu, and the various language options they represent, have arisen from the vision of the previous principal, Jim Laughton, and his desire to see the school curriculum reflect the ethnic diversity of the community it serves; (for a discussion of his influence, see Cazden, 1989; May, in press). The development of these innovative school structures has been closely allied with the expectations and participation of the local school community. Ethnic groups within the community are involved in curriculum decision-making and are drawn on for their cultural expertise in the development and, at times, teaching of resources (see below). The language immersion preschools, which are community run, provide direct links between the school and local ethnic groups, and many of their children go on to the bilingual ropu within the school. Parents are welcome to observe or participate in the ropu at any time, and often do so, while school functions are always strongly supported. This degree of parental involvement is the exception rather than the rule in most schools, but it is particularly unusual for ethnic minority parents, who often feel alienated by the school process. As Cazden observes in her study of Richmond Road; 'the front door [of the school] is indeed always open.' (1989: 158)

The relational commitment which whanau structures foster within the school is also seen in the collective approach to teaching that has been adopted by the staff. The largely open plan setting of the school allows for most of the ropu to be taught in 'shared spaces' and a principle of the school is that there always be two teachers in every room. This allows the ropu to be further divided into 'home groups'. Home groups are the basic teaching groups and it is the pupils in them that are monitored and reported on to parents by individual teachers. The presently favourable staff to student ratio sees these groups comprise approximately 20 pupils. However, the ropu can effectively operate with greatly increased numbers — as they have done in the past — because of the varied individual and collective teaching arrangements, and the variety of resources available at all levels (see below). The shared teaching and the instructional peer relationships characteristic of the ropu may, in fact, actually be inhibited by a lack of numbers because children of different ages and ability in the vertical groups are thinly spread.

The team teaching approach that the ropu structure demands requires a highly structured timetable so that pupils can become familiar with daily routines and can gain security from knowing what comes next. Pupils will know, for example, that at certain times each day they do particular activities. Each day may vary in what it offers, depending on the overall balance of the weekly programme, but children are always aware of what any given day holds for them. Hodson (1986) argues that children learn best in this type of secure environment where they can explore, test, share, communicate and develop their ideas in an atmosphere of trusted confidence. He goes on to suggest that teachers will best achieve a revolution in their own curriculum understanding and expertise if they adopt similar methods. This collectivity is very apparent in the staff of Richmond Road and it also encompasses the management of the school where the principal and the two associate principals work collaboratively as an administrative team. The associate principals rotate this responsibility — spending two weeks in a class which they share with another teacher, and two weeks in the office. This ensures that the administration does not lose touch with what is happening in the classroom and is aimed at preventing potential isolation between those who administer and those who teach in the school. Responsibility is shared and non-hierarchical relationships are emphasised. As the current principal, Lionel Pedersen, argues, the aim of the school is to break down pedagogical isolation — by rejecting artificial class grouping by age, and through shared administration and teaching.

This collaboration is closely allied with staff development generally and curriculum development in particular. The collective approach to teaching allows individual teachers to be released every morning to look at curriculum issues. Likewise, staff meetings — which are held every Tuesday after school and regularly continue into early evening — focus on co-operation and staff development. This involvement in curriculum development by staff is also supported through the organisation of staff into curriculum teams that deliberately cut across the ropu teaching teams. Curriculum teams develop resources for the curriculum during the course of the year (these resources must include all ethnic groups represented in the school community), supervise these materials, and provide support for staff working in other areas. The involvement of all staff in this process leads to a significant coherence and consistency across the curriculum and a great deal of mutual support among teachers (Cazden, 1989). Community participation is encouraged through an open door policy that allows for full community consultation and involvement in the discussion and development of curriculum policy.

The discussion of curriculum issues within the school is well established, wide-ranging and inclusive. As Marland suggests, a well informed staff (and, one might add, community) 'is able to respond to all issues within the total context of an institution ... and is able to participate in educational debate' (1977: 6). A knowledge of educational theory is regarded as the essential prerequisite to achieving this level of debate at Richmond Road. Pedersen, the principal, argues that there is no substitute for wide teacher knowledge and suggests that the result has been an enormous accumulation of knowledge among the staff on the nature and process of teaching. More than this though, it fosters the principle that teachers are learners also; if learners can learn, why can't teachers? What is emphasised as a result is process rather than product and this is exactly why, Pedersen suggests, the school has been able to successfully implement a whole-school language policy. Teachers have had a sufficient basis in theory to understand the educational intentions involved in language

25

policy development and have thus been able to fully implement them. Corson reiterates this point in discussing the difficulties of understanding the concept of 'language across the curriculum' (LAC):

> One answer to this problem for LAC is for teachers to be given greater access to theory, which is professional knowledge about the processes of language and learning, coupled with better information about what children can be expected to do and what they are doing in progressive settings. (1990: 84-85)

The result at Richmond Road is a critical pedagogy, as described by Smyth, which 'move[s] beyond theorising about our practice along the lines of 'this works for me' ... to ask questions instead about why we act as we do, and whose interests are served by continuing in this manner' (1989: 57). It has been a long process to get to this point and has had much to do with the previous principal, Jim Laughton, and his commitment, over a period of sixteen years, to establish this critically informed pedagogy within the school (see Cazden, 1989; May, 1994, for a fuller discussion). As Maybin (1985) notes, working through a language policy means talking about and working through curriculum change and this is neither a short nor easy process. Pedersen reiterates the difficulty of this process in his comment; 'if you believe that every child can progress, it's just the rates that differ, then teachers have got to believe that too and that was a very hard barrier ... to break down.'

The Rationale

The breaking down of structural barriers is central to Richmond Road's concern to contest the marginalisation of ethnic minority groups — and their languages — in education. The school recognises and endorses Bourdieu's observation that despite appearances of equality and universality the pedagogical tradition in most schools is only there for the benefit of pupils who are 'in the *particular position* of possessing a cultural heritage conforming to that demanded by the school.' (1974: 38) Bourdieu goes on to argue that the dominant form of language is reproduced in these schools, usually without opposition, because the notion of linguistic competence is divorced from the social and political conditions which legitimate its use (Thompson, 1984). It is this process and the relations of force implicit in it that Richmond Road consciously aims to resist by promoting the recognition, affirmation and celebration of cultural difference within the school. The role of language(s) is seen as central to achieving this aim, since as Bourdieu suggests, 'language is not only an instrument of communication or even of knowledge, but also an instrument of power' (1977; cited in Thompson, 1984: 46). However, it is also framed at Richmond Road within the broader context of respecting cultural autonomy and difference. As Pedersen argues, 'the school is about a way of living rather than just language. It is no use knowing the language at the expense of cultural tradition — all it becomes then is a translation, however fluent, of Pakeha culture.' The fostering of language is important but the cultural context which it represents, and from which it comes, should never be lost from sight. This accords with Colin Baker's observation that 'to support a language without supporting its attendant culture is to fund an expensive life-support machine attached to someone culturally dead or dying.' (1988: 100)

Bilingualism

The bilingual structure of the school is determined within this broader context. The children's use of their home language(s) is encouraged wherever possible within the school and, in the case of the Maori, Samoan and Cook Islands bilingual ropu, is formalised in a bilingual curriculum. The bilingual ropu are based on a dual-medium approach to language. During half of each morning and every other afternoon, the teachers speak only the home language to the children and the children are encouraged to respond in the same language. At other times, English is spoken. When the home language is in use, however, pupils are not required to speak the language prescribed if they do not wish to. As Cazden (1989) observes, this might be a weakness of the programmes since low-status languages such as these need as much support as possible within the school to avoid being swamped beyond it. The school's approach is, however, consistent with its broader conception of the role of language(s) in the fostering of cultural identity. It also accords with the identification of choice as a crucial variable in the success of bilingual programmes (see Baker, 1988; Cummins, 1983; Holmes, 1984) and simply extends that notion to include children as well as parents and the wider community. Moreover, the bilingual ethos of the school clearly endorses a maintenance rather than a transitional view of bilingual education (see Appel & Muysken, 1987; Baker, 1988; & Romaine, 1989). As the previous principal, Laughton,

27

eloquently argues, 'bilingual education ... wisely conceived — [can] make a difference — as an act of respect and humility by the powerful, as an expression of confidence and determination by the powerless, [and] as an exercise in genuine communication among all.' (1985a: 1) The importance of bilingualism permeates the language philosophy of the school. Language and culture are regarded as an area of strength and competency for all children and the teachers recognise and acknowledge Ken Goodman's observation that if as teachers they undermine a child's language they also undermine that child's ability to learn (Richmond Road School, 1983).

Policy Development

These intentions are supported, as we have seen, by a dynamic and relational approach to policy development. The democratic policy development that characterises the school involves both teachers and parents in decisions about the language needs of the school and operates within the wider language expectations of the local community. Richmond Road has recognised the need for schools to reduce the social distance between themselves and the communities they serve by involving parents in school policy making. As Corson suggests, 'schools collaboratively managed [in this way] and with agreed and working policies are more likely to be places of staff and community commitment' (1990: 59). Maybin (1985) also observes that schools which have made a firm commitment to work more closely with parents have found an enormous range of activities is possible in the implementation of a language policy. The result sees the adoption at Richmond Road of a whole-school language policy which recognises the close relationship between the languages that students use, their identity, and their culture. Moreover, these connections are actively fostered and given expression through the structures of the school.

Ropu

One of these pivotal structures is the vertical whanau or ropu grouping established within the school by Jim Laughton. Laughton saw such groupings as a means of giving 'institutionalised power' to ethnic minority children who might otherwise not have had access to it in a society where dominant power relations are perpetuated through schooling (Richmond Road School, 1986). His aim was to increase their alternatives through the ropu structure: by increasing the age and ability range with which children were in contact; by providing children with opportunities to experience a variety of roles and to develop an appropriate range of social skills; and by assisting the growth of self respect through the recognition of ethnic diversity and the wide range of skills, interests and cultural perspectives children would bring to the group as a whole. Such an organisation, he argued, gives more power and choices to everyone. There is more room for independence but this is paralleled by the expectation that responsibility towards the whole group be accepted:

> inherent within the whanau organisation is the integration of belief systems which emphasise group rather than individual values. If cultural maintenance is to be a priority at Richmond Road School then stress must be placed on values which contribute to the strength of the group as a whole rather than on those which are individualistic. This kind of system is necessary to support cultural transmission in the curriculum. (Richmond Road School, 1986: 3)

This means that cultural features which emphasise collectivism take precedence over those which are individualistic, thus forming the basis for the characteristic ethos of the school — co-operation rather than competition. Acceptance of this kind of responsibility is inherent in family group organisation; socially, by demonstrating care for others, and educationally through peer support activities such as paired reading. The latter activity, for example, sees children with competency at one reading level involved in working with children who are at other stages of development. This encourages the growth of skills which will lead to independence within a supportive, co-operative environment and is consistent with the values of the minority cultures of many of the students. Individualism is not diminished within this approach. Rather, individualism as *competitive isolation* — a peculiarly western conception — is re-conceptualised within the broader context of mutual accountability:

> Family grouping ... rests on the idea of integration of differences — differences of ethnicity, age, ability, gender, interest and knowledge. These factors are brought together so children may grow in knowledge, appreciation and respect for themselves and others .... they are encouraged to take responsibility for their own learning and [to] support the learning process of those around them. (Richmond Road School, 1986: 4).

29

Resources

In order for this to occur children need access to resources they can use independently and collaboratively. Ready made resources are available at Richmond Road in the form of 'boxed books' and 'fluency kits'. The boxed book system consists of sets of graded reading material from 5-11 years which are issued to ropu on a fortnightly basis. Those with reading ages above 11 years are expected to use other sources such as the school library or public library for their reading. Fluency kits are boxes of books which are designed for beginning readers who are experiencing difficulties at their assigned reading level. The kits provide a range of reading formats and are designed to be used in silent reading at approximately two levels below the child's instructional level.

However, for the most part resources are developed by teachers within the school, particularly through the development of 'focus' resources. Focus resources are developed by each curriculum team. They are a set of social studies and associated curriculum resources 'focused' by the exploration of a particular concept. Teachers prepare these resources at ten levels of reading independence and in four learning contexts (see below). The reading levels match the material to the students while the learning contexts facilitate their wide-ranging, interactive and open ended use. Children are able to explore and investigate ideas in a variety of different ways, either individually or co-operatively, and according to their own style, preference and interest. If a child at one level of literacy, for example, wants access to resource material at a higher level, she or he can negotiate with another child at the appropriate level of literacy for any activity. Each child knows his or her own level of reading independence and those of others within the ropu because the information is displayed on charts — not, as in many cases, as a means of ranking but, rather, as a means of identifying for children whom they can go to for support and whom they can assist.

Learning Arrangements

The learning arrangements which underpin the resources used at Richmond Road comprise: superior/inferior, co-operative, collaborative and independent.

Superior/inferior arrangements are those which usually characterise the school curriculum. One person, who is almost always the teacher, conveys information to those who lack it, the pupils. Richmond Road accepts that superior/inferior arrangements are a part of educational life but does not endorse the notion that the teacher should always occupy the former position. A pupil or a parent may be recognised as having expertise in a particular field (such as a particular language or culture) which they can be called upon to share in the classroom. The contrast between these two approaches is captured nicely by R. S. Peters' (1973) distinction between 'assigned' and 'provisional' authority. Assigned authority focuses on the responsibility of the teacher to dispense knowledge while provisional authority is described by Peters as that held by the person 'who knows the most' in a given situation. As Cazden observes, 'whoever has knowledge [at Richmond Road] teaches.' (1989: 151)

Co-operative arrangements put children into shared situations where they support each other while completing a task. These groups are usually self chosen and encompass a wide range of skills and ability. They foster the notion of co-operation rather than competition and aim to reduce children's fear of failure through an active participation in a supportive system which demands corporate rather than individual accountability.

Collaborative arrangements bring children together in situations which require shared understanding because those involved have different information that they are required to put together to complete a task. This involves children in the sharing of information, the negotiation of meaning, and debate, until consensus is reached. Children are free to express a wide range of their own ideas, beliefs, values and attitudes in order to produce a shared conclusion, although it is the process of negotiation rather than the eventual outcome which is emphasised.

Independent arrangements allow every child the opportunity to operate individually at her or his own speed and level, with materials suited to individual needs and interests. In this way, independence is developed and the child is encouraged to take responsibility for her or his own learning. This learning is still, however, tied to the underlying principle of co-operation because it aims to encourage the acceptance of responsibility for knowledge already held, rather than independent learning at the expense of others.

Encompassing all the various learning strategies are resource materials designed to introduce concepts, theme approaches and base stories to the whole group. This gives the coherence and continuity necessary for drawing together the variety of activities in which children can be involved.

Language Experience

'Language experience' is another central tenet of the school's language programme. It aims to contextualise and integrate language activities — emphasising meaning rather than form — and involves children in developing and expanding language in the context of experiences, books and/or events. For example, children discuss an event or experience which is recorded in written form by the teacher (a chart or wall story is often used) and then the children read back what has been written. In a ropu, which encompasses a range of backgrounds and experiences, this process provides a common experience with which children can identify. Reading the material back to the teacher is facilitated by a written form of language familiar to the children and the difficulties associated with using school texts, which tend to exclude the languages and cultures of minority pupils, are avoided.

Writing

Richmond Road's approach to written language incorporates similar ideals and strategies. Koch's (1982) description of the writing process as 'learned terror' for many children is recognised as characteristic of many approaches to writing in schools, and is specifically avoided by Richmond Road. Emphasis is placed, instead, on making writing fun. Writing is de-emphasised as a separate activity and encouraged as a necessary part of other curriculum activities in accordance with the principle of language experience. Closely allied to this is the recognition of children as experts in the writing process. The different cultural, linguistic and personal responses children incorporate into learning to write — and the experimentation necessarily involved in such a process — are encouraged. Concomitantly, the notion of teaching a 'correct' writing model is discounted. As a result, a variety of writing activities are employed: private writing, supported writing, and co-operative writing.

Private writing is characterised by little, if any, teacher correction. Children are encouraged to express themselves freely in writing and to view writing, accordingly, as an effective means of personal communication. A time is set aside each day for writing of this kind which is not corrected and is only shared at the child's discretion. Private writing can also include pre-writing or rehearsal which emphasises for children the developmental nature of the writing process.

Supported writing involves providing a framework for writing such as the retelling of favourite stories, the completion of stories or the writing of stories from a different point of view. Whatever framework is adopted, however, support is always available to the children when required.

Co-operative writing sees children working together in accomplishing a task which includes written work.

All these writing varieties (along with those established for reading) are employed in the construction and use of curriculum resources.

Monitoring

The accurate matching of instructional materials to the child's level of reading competence is an essential prerequisite for all these learning arrangements and requires ongoing monitoring to ensure that accurate matching does occur. For example, regular oversight of individual reading is maintained within home groups and running records of children's reading progress are kept. These records include not only reading levels but also skills or cues used, needed, or misused. Movement from one reading level to the next requires children to meet stringent criteria. The instructional level — where a child reads fluently, independently and with understanding — requires 95% accuracy with at least a 1:3 self correction rate. The easy reading level (for library and taking home) requires 98-100% accuracy.

Laughton, the previous principal, argues that the monitoring process can determine this because it 'entails observation of behaviour in familiar contexts using familiar processes, [but is] often focused on unfamiliar content' (1985b: 1). Its purpose is to find out how the pupil operates, and the function of familiarity 'is to facilitate access to underlying competence, imperfectly reflected at best in the student's performance' (*ibid*). Laughton goes on to advocate that monitoring should, as a result, replace testing as the principal form of assessment in schools. He suggests that the latter is more concerned with finding out what a student does *not* know and is, as such, intrinsically less effective in gauging the competencies and skills of students. Historically, also, assessment based on testing has played the role of legitimising the disabling of ethnic minority students (Cummins, 1986).

The Policy

Richmond Road demonstrates the kind of environment in which a whole-school language policy can flourish. The school's language policy is representative and inclusive of all the ethnic groups within the school. It has arisen out of a close consultation with all ethnic groups in the local community (including the majority Pakeha group). It is specifically concerned to empower all children by recognising and giving status to the languages they bring to the school, and by recognising and encouraging their development for the benefit of the whole school and wider community. It has resulted in traditional grouping by age being replaced by vertical language-based ropu which are pluralist and non-assimilative; recognising and respecting cultural differences. It demonstrates non-hierarchical and collaborative relationships between staff and has involved, and continues to involve, teachers in their own processes of change.

Richmond Road's holistic approach has meant that, until recently, policies pertaining to language have been dispersed through various school documents. The policy document outlined below then is my own interpretation; (for a more extensive outline of school policies at Richmond Road, see May, 1994). Other examples of recent school language policies can be found in Corson (1990).

34

RICHMOND ROAD SCHOOL: AN HOLISTIC LANGUAGE POLICY

The following policy articulates the current position of Richmond Road School in its approach to the place of language(s) within the school. It needs to be recognised that this position is not a static one. It has developed to this point over a period of twenty years and continues to be evaluated against the real world of the school and adjusted accordingly. This 'critically informed action' (see Carr & Kemmis, 1983; Kemmis and McTaggart, 1988) also accords with the school's aim to create 'self-sustaining self-improving systems' and to place more importance on process than on product (Richmond Road School, 1983).

In implementing these ideas certain values are prerequisite: difference is never equated with deficiency; co-operation is fostered not competition; cultural respect is seen as essential to developing a pluralistic society; and the school's function is directed towards increasing a child's options rather than changing them. Such a conception also highlights the arbitrariness of detailing a 'language' policy since the fostering of language(s) cannot be separated from the cultural context from which it springs nor from the type of society one would wish to see result. Richmond Road locates its view of the role of languages in the school within a wider frame of reference; that of recognising and affirming cultural respect, autonomy and difference through the structures of the school. The following policies attempt to reflect this aim:

Nau te rourou, Naku te rourou
Ka ora te tangata

Your food basket, My food basket
Will give life to the people

1.   Introduction

1.1   *The school remains committed to fostering cultural pluralism through the recognition, inclusion and maintenance of languages other than that of the majority group; both within the curriculum, and in the life of the school generally.*

1.2   *The basis of any further policy development must continue to reflect the dynamic language needs of the school and the language expectations of the wider school community.*

1.3   *Policy development will continue to be based on a process of collaborative and informed decision-making by staff and management, in close consultation with the community.*

2.   School Organisation and Management

2.1   Organisational Objectives

2.1.1   *The organisational policy of the school is based on the following tenets:*

   i)   *To increase the age and ability range of organised groups of students;*

   ii)   *To encourage teacher commitment to individual students by increasing length of association;*

   iii)   *To provide for greater common purpose among teachers by reducing the classification categories of the school;*

   iv)   *To institute a pattern of delegation which emphasises responsibility for individual students throughout their schooling.*

2.2   School and Ropu Organisation

2.2.1   *In 1994, the school comprised five ropu or family groups. Ropu 1, which remains solely English medium; Ropu 2, which now incorporates the Cook Islands bilingual unit; Ropu 3, which includes the Samoan bilingual unit; Ropu 4, the Maori bilingual unit; and Ropu 5, the Inner City Language Unit.*

2.2.2   *All ropu cover the full age range of New Entrant to Form 2 (5-13 yrs.)*

2.3   Staffing

2.3.1   *Criteria for the selection of staff to the school should include:*

   i)   *An applicant's willingness to learn the systems in operation at Richmond Road;*

   ii)   *The applicant's willingness to negotiate a broader meaning than the usual authoritative and transmissionist role of the teacher;*

   iii)   *Whether the applicant's appointment to the staff will increase its diversity and/or more closely reflect the school population.*

2.4   Staff Development

2.4.1   *The programme of staff development will continue along the established lines of weekly teacher release, resource develop-*

ment in curriculum focus teams and training opportunities at staff meetings and special in-service days.

2.4.2 The goals of staff development remain the furthering of staff knowledge in the curriculum, management and organisation of the school; the sharing of this with the wider community; and the engendering, through this process, of the key components of cultural maintenance and access to power in a learning environment for adults and children.

2.5 Resources

2.5.1 Curriculum teams will continue to provide 'focus resources' at ten reading levels and for use in four learning modes: superior/inferior, co-operative, collaborative, and independent.

2.5.2 Reading materials ('boxed books' and 'fluency kits') will continue to be maintained and developed.

2.6 Community Consultation and Involvement

2.6.1 All school and curriculum policy decisions are to be developed in consultation with the school community.

2.6.2 The co-option of kaumatua (Maori elders) and Pacific Island leaders onto the Board of Trustees (school management body) acknowledges the reciprocal relationship between the school and community.

2.6.3 Board of Trustees meetings are to be held regularly and all community members can attend and participate. All decisions are to be arrived at by consensus by those in attendance as this constitutes the major forum for official community consultation.

2.6.4 The involvement of parents, either formally or informally, in the life of the school is a continuing priority.

3. The Curriculum

3.1 Bilingual Education

3.1.1 The bilingual ropu are based on a maintenance principle of dual-language medium instruction which aims to maintain and enrich the home languages of minority children through the school system.

3.1.2 Bilingual curriculum options are to be extended where possible. In 1991, for example, a Cook Islands dual-medium bilingual unit was established in addition to the Maori and Samoan units. The next bilingual option it is hoped will be a Tongan one.

3.1.3 Parental choice concerning the involvement of children in these programmes is seen as critical to their success.

3.1.4 The notion of choice should be extended to the pupils within these programmes who may be encouraged, but should not be coerced, into speaking the language prescribed.

3.2 Language Experience and Reading

3.2.1 A principle underlying the reading/language programme is that of 'language experience' where children are encouraged to develop and expand language in the context of experiences, books or events.

3.2.2 Establishing the instructional level appropriate to the child's reading ability is regarded as essential to fostering competence in reading.

i) Children should be matched at their reading levels not their age level.

ii) Regular oversight of individual reading needs to be maintained, at least once a term with all children and more often for lower levels. Running records on all children are to be kept.

iii) The instructional level should be at 95% accuracy with at least 1:3 self correction rate. Easy reading level should be at 98-100%.

iv) Peer support should be encouraged, particularly through paired reading, to complement the support given by the teacher.

v) Accurate matching, careful monitoring, and teacher and peer support should develop confident and competent readers.

3.2.3 Reading materials (boxed books and fluency kits) are available for children with reading ages under 11 years. The school library is available for children with reading ages over 11 years.

3.3 Written Language

3.3.1 Writing is encouraged as a necessary part of other curriculum activities as well as an activity in itself.

3.3.2 A variety of writing activities are encouraged: private writing, supported writing; and co-operative writing.

3.3.3 *Children are to be regarded as experts in the writing process. The notion of teaching a 'correct' model of writing is discounted and experimentation in children's writing encouraged.*

4. Conclusion

4.1 *The language policy will continue to be revised yearly as part of the ongoing curriculum development established within the school.*

4.2 *The revision process will continue to recognise and incorporate developments in language theory and the changing needs and circumstances of the school.*

Conclusion

While it is not suggested that this particular school model be explicitly followed, Richmond Road does illustrate how the formulation and implementation of school-based curriculum development, in the form of an LPAC, can be effectively achieved by the school. Returning to Skilbeck's (1984) observations on school-based curriculum development, it is clear that Richmond Road School is a relational school. The pursuit and application of curriculum innovation and development in language policy has led to a fundamental restructuring of the school. This change in school organisational structure and pedagogical practice has been based on collaborative decision-making at a staff level and an open interchange between the school and its community with regard to the language needs of its pupils. There has been a recognition in all of this of the political motivation and role of the school in working to this end. As Pedersen states, 'a whole [school] language policy has to be about whole life; about social and political structure and change: otherwise it's a waste of time.'

All of these aspects, taken together, attempt to actualise Richmond Road School's concern to break the cycle of marginalisation for ethnic minority groups in schooling. The development of an holistic and inclusive language policy at the school demonstrates the truth of Cummins' assertion that 'widespread failure does not occur in minority groups that are positively oriented towards both their own and the dominant culture, that do not perceive themselves as inferior to the dominant group, and that are not alienated from their own cultural values' (1986: 22). Such educational initiative and innovation augur well for the possibilities of change, both for minority children and for those wishing to integrate the theory of 'language policies across the curriculum' with the practices of schools. The demands on schools — organisationally, pedagogically and relationally — may be great, but Richmond Road shows that it can be done.

Bibliography

Appel, R. & Muysken, P. (1987). *Language contact and bilingualism.* London: Edward Arnold.

Baker, C. (1988). *Key issues in bilingualism and bilingual education.* Clevedon: Multilingual Matters.

Bourdieu, P. (1974). The school as a conservative force: Scholastic and cultural inequalities. In J. Eggleston (Ed.). *Contemporary research in the sociology of education.* London: Methuen, 32-46.

Carr, W. Kemmis, S. (1983). *Becoming critical: Knowing through action research.* Victoria: Deakin University Press.

Cazden, C. (1989). Richmond Road: A multilingual/multicultural primary school in Auckland, New Zealand. *Language and Education: An International Journal, 3,* 143-166.

Corson, D. (1990). *Language policy across the curriculum.* Clevedon: Multilingual Matters.

Cummins, J. (1983). *Heritage Language Foundation. A literature review.* Ontario Ministry of Education.

Cummins, J. (1986). Empowering minority students: A framework for intervention. *Harvard Educational Review, 56,* 18-36.

Hodson, D. (1986). Towards a model for school-based curriculum development. *Delta 38.* Palmerston North: Department of Education, Massey University, 29-35.

Holmes, J. (1984). *Bilingual education.* Occasional Publication 11. Wellington: Victoria University English Language Institute.

Kemmis, S. McTaggart, R. (Eds.). (1988). *The action research planner* (3rd ed.). Deakin: Deakin University Press.

Koch, R. (1982). Syllogisms and superstitions: The current state of responding to writing. *Language Arts, 59,* 464-471.

Laughton, J. (1985a). Maori bilingual option. Richmond Road School Working Paper.

Laughton, J. (1985b). Assessment. Richmond Road School Working Paper.

Marland, M. (1977). *Language across the curriculum.* London: Heinemann.

May, S. (1991). Making the difference for minority children: The development of an holistic language policy at Richmond Road School, Auckland, New Zealand. *Language, Culture and Curriculum, 4,* 201-217.

May, S. (1993). Redeeming multicultural education. *Language Arts, 70,* 364-372.

May, S. (1994). *Making multicultural education work*. Clevedon: Multilingual Matters.

Maybin, J. (1985). Working towards a school language policy. In *Every child's language: An in-service pack for primary teachers*. Clevedon: The Open University & Multilingual Matters, 95-108.

Peters, R. (Ed.). (1973). *The philosophy of education*. London: Oxford University Press.

Richmond Road School (1983). Learning and teaching in multi-cultural settings. Seminar given at Auckland Teachers College by Principal and Staff.

Richmond Road School (1986). Cultural diversity: Challenge and response. Richmond Road School Working Paper.

Romaine, S. (1989). *Bilingualism*. Oxford: Basil Blackwell.

Skilbeck, M. (1984). *School-based curriculum development*. London: Harper & Row.

Smyth, W. (1989). A critical pedagogy of classroom practice: Education reform at the chalkface. *Delta 41*. Palmerston North: Department of Education, Massey University, 53-64.

Stenhouse, L. (1975). *An introduction to curriculum research and development*. London: Heinemann.

Thompson, J. (1984). *Studies in the theory of ideology*. Cambridge: Polity Press.

Chapter 3

'We can't tell our stories in English': Language, Story and Culture in the Primary School

Adrian Blackledge

Introduction

Children in British schools speak more than two hundred languages. As many as five hundred thousand children learn to speak a language other than English at home before they encounter English at school. It has long been recognised that children's primary learning medium is their first language. Yet at policy-making level there has been scant recognition of these other languages of Britain, of their immense value as a resource, or of the crucial part they have to play in the education of bilingual children. Still less have governments encouraged teachers to promote the development of children's languages in the classroom, preferring to turn a deaf ear to the voices of more than half a million children.

This chapter arises from my experience as a teacher in the multilingual primary classroom. In the course of developing bilingual education strategies I became aware that bilingual children's work would sometimes improve dramatically when they used their home language. This was particularly evident when children were telling stories to each other in their own languages. Research findings elsewhere have suggested the cognitive benefits of home language work with very young children coming to English for the first time. This chapter suggests that bilingual children benefit from home language work in the classroom when they are already competent users of English, and that the value of children's home language lies not only in terms of linguistic/cognitive increment, but as part of a broad provision of multicultural/antiracist education.

'I only speak to my parents and grandpa and grandma in Mirpuri'

In a large, multilingual school in Birmingham children from Year 6 (10-11 years) told stories to children from Year 3 (7-8 years) in homogeneous linguistic groups. During a series of weekly storytelling sessions, stories were told in Sylheti, Mirpuri and Malay. Some groups of bilingual children were asked to tell their stories in English. All children were then asked to write one of their stories in English. It soon became clear that most of the children telling stories in their first language were relating tales which originated in the narrative wealth of their home culture. In the course of this work children discussed their experiences of telling and listening to stories. The following is a transcript of part of a conversation with four Mirpuri-speaking girls in Year 6.

Teacher: Where do your stories come from?

Shakila: My grandma tells me stories, she came from Pakistan and tells me all the Pakistani stories.

T.: And which language do you prefer to use to retell those stories? Do you tell them best in Mirpuri?

Shakila: No, it doesn't matter. It depends who I am telling it to I suppose. If I was telling it to a teacher, or to Saima, I would use English. If I was telling it to my little brother, he's four and doesn't know English really yet, I would use Mirpuri.

T: But you don't think you tell the story better in Mirpuri, even though it is told to you in Mirpuri?

Shakila: No, it's just who I'm talking to.

44

T: What about you two — do you prefer to tell stories in English or Mirpuri?

Noreen: I think English, because I can explain them better in English.

Sabrina: Yes, I think so, too. You can explain the stories better in English.

T: Even if the stories are told to you in Mirpuri?

Sabrina: Yes, even when my aunt or grandma tells me a story in Mirpuri, I can tell it better in English, because I usually hear more stories in English.

T: What about you, Saika, which language do you prefer to use to tell stories?

Saika: I don't know, it doesn't matter. I can tell it the same in both.

T: You don't think, like Noreen and Sabrina, that you tell stories better in English?

Saika: No. I don't think so.

T: The story you told today, where did you first hear it, and in which language?

Saika: My grandma told it to me in Mirpuri. She doesn't speak English.

T: Is it still just as easy to tell that story in English as in Mirpuri?

Saika: Yes, it's the same.

Savva (1990) reminds us that 'bilingual children's language experience is not the same: each of them has a different linguistic background'. The four girls in this conversation apparently have very similar linguistic histories — each born in Britain to Mirpuri-speaking parents and educated at the same school from the age of four — yet they have different perceptions of their abilities to tell sophisticated stories in their first language. While Saika and Shakila feel that they have equal narrative facility in Mirpuri and English, Noreen and Sabrina have a different view of their storytelling skills in the two languages. Noreen and Sabrina both feel that they are better able to 'explain' their story in English than in Mirpuri. This perception of their language preferences raises an important question: are Noreen and Sabrina's narrative skills (and therefore, by implication, other language skills) being *replaced* by the skills they are learning in English? Levine (1990) emphasises the importance of a dialectical relationship between the languages children already know and their becoming adept in the new one:

> it is our hope, and what we work for, that English will become an *additional,* not a displacing language in our pupils' lives.

If English is to replace rather than add to the languages of the children we teach, we must ask what is the effect of such a programme on their cultural identity, their self-esteem and sense of their place in the community. The monolingual teacher can do much to encourage an additive rather than a subtractive bilingual environment; that is, a classroom environment in which children are *adding* a new language to their existing skills rather than *replacing* their first language with that of the school. A bilingual education programme will be successful if the school actively promotes the value and use of children's languages. The curriculum need not be taught through those languages. If children are encouraged to use their languages at their convenience, and these languages are accorded genuine value in the classroom, it is likely that existing and new languages will develop side-by-side. Cummins (1986) shows that the development of a positive multilingual classroom currently resides in the hands of mono-lingual professionals: 'An additive orientation does not require the actual teaching of the minority language'. If schools are positive in their attitude to, and use of languages, then children's learning need not be hindered by their bilingualism.

Cummins and Swain (1986) provide evidence from a range of bilingual education programmes to show that experience with either first or second language can promote development of the linguistic proficiency under-lying both languages. Skills learned in one language will transfer readily to another. Thus if children speak in their home language for part of the curriculum they are not wasting time that could be spent 'learning Eng-lish'. In fact their development of skills in the home language enables them to learn English more proficiently and with greater sophistication. Children are able to add a new language to their existing skills when their first language is strongly reinforced by a committed bilingual education programme in the school.

Outside the school gates bilingual children use different languages according to their context. The children in our study said they spoke their home language (Sylheti, Mirpuri, Hindi or Malay) and English at home; for most of the children this meant usually speaking in English to siblings, and in the home language to parents, grandparents and other members of the family or community. Noreen (Y3, Mirpuri), for example, typically explains: 'To my mum and dad I speak Mirpuri — my dad knows English a bit. To my sisters and brother I speak English because they don't like Mirpuri a lot'.

Most of the fifty children in our study were aware of using languages at the mosque which they rarely used elsewhere, e.g. Urdu for instruction, Arabic for reading the Quran. All of the children said they used English and the home language at school; many added that they used English in the classroom, and the home language mainly in the playground. Although most of the children said they hear stories in English and the home language, a majority said they prefer to tell stories in English. However, almost all of the children qualified this by saying, as Shakera (Sylheti) does, that their language of narrative depends on their audience:

> If I tell it to someone who speaks my language I would tell it in my language because they won't understand the words that are hard for that person. So it would be easy in my language for them.

This awareness of the linguistic abilities of the audience was commmon among the children's responses. Shazma (Y6, Mirpuri) is representative of the majority: 'I think I prefer to tell stories in English because some words I cannot say in Mirpuri so I prefer English'. Most of the children said English was their most proficient language, while fewer said their home language was the one they spoke best. Saika's (Y6) response was typical:

> I think that I speak in English the best because I speak to my sisters and brothers in English and my cousins speak to me in English too. I only speak to my parents and grandpa and grandma in Mirpuri.

Shakera (Y6) found a different explanation for her perception that English was becoming her stronger language: 'because I have been in this country more than Bangladesh and I haven't been in Bangladeshi schools so I haven't learnt much'. Almost all of the children said they learned the home language first, as a young child. A majority of the children said they thought it was important to use their home language. Saika's response was again representative: 'Well! I think your first language is more important than your second language because you can learn quickly from your parents'.

The most immediately striking aspect of the children's conversation is their positive attitude to their languages. Most of the children feel that their languages should be retained, do have value and are a valid medium of learning. At the same time, however, they feel that English is, or is becoming, their stronger language. What are the implications here for the classroom? Is it sufficient for children to be allowed to have their languages at home and in the community, but to concentrate solely on English in the classroom? If we aim to teach the whole child, if we want to provide the fullest opportunities for children, it is essential to make use of the full range of their learning resources. For bilingual children this means enabling them to use their home languages when and how they choose. Savva (1990) insists that we take every opportunity to ensure that the curriculum 'both reflects and makes use of the linguistic diversity in our schools and the rest of society'. Only by placing linguistic diversity at the centre of our classroom planning and organisation will we provide real choice for children in their language use.

'We can't tell our stories in English'

The following conversation occurred when a group of Sylheti children were asked to use only English in telling stories to each other. They had barely begun the storytelling session when they came to me in some distress:

Teacher: Is something wrong?

Shakera: We can't tell our stories in English because it's too difficult, we don't know all the words.

T.:   What do you mean?

Fahima: Sir, we are telling Bengali stories but we don't know them in English. Can we speak Bengali (meaning Sylheti) please?

T: You know that usually I am very happy for you to speak Sylheti whenever you like, but would you please use English just for this work?

Amin: Oh, Sir, but Bodrul's group is speaking Sylheti.

T: I know it doesn't seem fair, but perhaps another week you can choose which language to use. Why do you prefer to use Sylheti?

Fahima: Because in Sylheti there's more sentences that we need for our story.

Amin: Yes, Sir, because they're Bengali stories.

T.: I see. Where did you hear the stories?

Shakera: From my grandma, she always tells us stories.

T: She tells them in Sylheti?

Shakera: Yes, Sir. I will tell the story in English if I have to, but I'll have to use some Bengali words.

Amin: But we won't be able to tell the real story, we can't really do it.

T: All right, go and see how you get on.

The children went away to tell their stories in mainly English, with a sprinkling of Sylheti words. The concern of the Sylheti group that they would not be able to tell their story effectively in English raises a number of questions. For these children the story could not be recreated in English. To deny children their language, as on this occasion we did, was to deny them their story; to deny them their story was to deny this part of their culture access to the classroom. The children's frustration was manifest. It may be that they felt aggrieved because they saw their peers telling stories using the appropriate language. These children are commonly encouraged to use their home language in the classroom. Other children in other schools may simply expect to be denied their language and culture, and live with the frustration. What does the children's reaction suggest to us about the place of home language for a group of competent users of English? Here is the same Sylheti group:

T.:   How did you get on with your story?

Shakera :   It would have been a better story if we had used Bengali.

Amin :   I missed out bits of my story because I had to tell it in English.

T.:   Do you think you tell stories better in English or Sylheti?

Shakera: Sylheti, because it's better in Sylheti, you can tell all the story.

During another session the groups of children were given pictures to stimulate their storytelling. These varied from scenes from traditional (European) folk tales to abstract modern art. The first thing to strike us was the fact that several of the bilingual groups responded to this activity by talking in English rather than home language. This was true whether they were discussing ideas or telling narrative. When reminded of the instructions, they moved back into home language. The children who started to speak in English rather than home language were choosing a language appropriate to the context. Whereas previously they had simply been asked to 'tell a story', this activity was one in which they were less required to draw on their cultural resources; the stimulus was provided by the (English) teacher, so they expected, even perhaps preferred to speak in English. This raises important questions for the classroom: to what extent should teachers insist that children use their home languages in curriculum work? How do we know whether children are genuinely making a choice of language, or are fitting in to the norm of the 'English' school? All bilinguals have a preferred and a second language for every discrete area of experience (Dodson, 1985). The children's perception of the activity in hand was that it was most appropriately managed in English rather than home language. Bilingual children will speak in English for curriculum activities unless positively encouraged to do otherwise. If a school does not genuinely promote an additive orientation towards bilingualism through use of language and culture in the curriculum, and a pedagogy which makes full use of children's existing skills, bilingual children will be likely to use the dominant language of the school for all activities except when specifically asked to use home language. If children understand that their languages are regarded by the school as peripheral, those languages will remain silent. The occasional storytelling session in home language is not a genuine and full role for children's languages in their learning. Children revert to English because they do not have a genuine choice of using their preferred language; the language of the school is English. We will only enable children to use their strongest or preferred language when we make those languages part of the legitimate learning medium of the classroom. This does not, of course, require all teachers to speak all languages; it does require all teachers of bilingual children to provide opportunities for their use in the mainstream curriculum.

The stories of the children who did use home language exemplified the positive steps that can be taken on the road to additive bilingual policy. We recorded on cassette the Mirpuri stories of Shakila and Umar; both children display an enthusiasm and fluency which have immense value in the development of narrative skills. If we accept the notion of linguistic interdependence (Cummins and Swain, 1986) this kind of work can only lead to enhanced narrative skills in English.

Monolingual teachers may be frustrated or even threatened by children using languages they can't understand. It is impossible for most teachers to assess children's talk when they are using their home languages. Of course we do not assess children all the time. When we want to assess their spoken English we can either arrange children in heterogeneous linguistic groups, or ask them to speak in English. It is essential that we do not deny children their natural learning medium simply because we can't always tell what they are saying. Shan (1990) suggests that monolingual teachers may be able to develop assessment skills to record the child's whole linguistic competence, but finally concedes that genuine assessment of bilingual children is only possible by the bilingual teacher; it is of utmost importance that multilingual teaching staff are trained and recruited to the classroom.

The arguments that bilingual children should learn either entirely in their first language or entirely in the majority language throughout their schooling are naive and misplaced. All schools must develop working policy which aims to teach English to the full potential of each child, while actively valuing and using the linguistic diversity of its community. If children are to learn effectively through a bilingual education programme, they must learn in an environment that is positive about their languages and actively encourages them to be multilingual. Not only should teachers support children's languages, but also their community and culture: in short, their identity. Savva (1990) shows that the very worst thing we can do is to deny children the wholeness of their linguistic and cultural experience. Their languages must be genuinely valued and supported by the school, and have a legitimate role in their learning. If children's languages are only allowed into the classroom occasionally, as an optional extra, children will understand that the school is interested in them only on its own terms. If racism is not actively opposed, or if children's cultural background is ignored, the gulf between school and home will remain. Children do not separate their language from their cultural identity; it would surely be a mistake for teachers to attempt to do so. Savva reminds us that 'bilingualism isn't only a language issue; it's also a race issue' (1990). Tansley (1986) acknowledges that widespread provision of home language teaching is unlikely in this country in the near future, and suggests that this should not prevent the committed teacher from becoming the 'linchpin' linking bilingual teachers and other bilingual staff in the school, providing a point of contact for community language teachers, parents and other representatives from minority communities. Thus the teacher becomes the co-ordinator of all those concerned with the education of bilingual children. In this way the class teacher, and indeed the school, can extend their bilingual education policy beyond the confines of the curriculum to incorporate the learning of the whole child.

'I think I speak the best in both languages'

Children were asked to tell a story to their group in response to the introduction of two colourful puppets recently brought from India. Each group was asked to use their strongest or preferred language. It was immediately notable that all of the eight Mirpuri groups used either English or, commonly, a combination of English and Mirpuri. As part of this mixing of codes, children would use both languages within a single sentence, and would also switch from one language to the other in separate sentences. Characteristically, Y6 children were less likely to use Mirpuri than Y3 children. The older group used the home language when explaining a point to the younger children, but used it less often when speaking to each other. The Sylheti groups told stories in Sylheti, and the Malaysian groups told stories in Malay before writing in English. A small number of children wrote, or attempted to write in their community languages. Arfan wrote his story in Urdu while Siti wrote her story in Malay.

LANGUAGE, STORY AND CULTURE IN THE PRIMARY SCHOOL

There is little evidence to support the notion that when bilingual children switch from one language to another they are interfering with their language development. Switching from one language to another is, rather, the norm for bilingual children, who do so as a matter of convenience. Mirpuri-speaking children in this group often used English for narrative, and Mirpuri to explain a difficult point, or to make clear something that had been misunderstood. In this case not only were the children taking account of their audience, they were using language according to its very specific context. Romaine (1989) suggests that rather than using the term 'interference' to describe this switching between languages, the more positive 'cross-linguistic influence' would be more appropriate:

> There is increasing evidence to indicate that this mixed mode of speaking serves important functions in the communities where it is used and that it is not random. (1989)

Romaine states that there is a clear relationship between language choice and social context. In her study of the Panjabi community in England she found a high degree of bilingualism, within which languages were regularly mixed, but without apparently harmful consequences. If we create a classroom environment which is committed to bilingualism we will enable children to use their languages freely and interdependently, thus opening up the classroom culturally and linguistically (Savva, 1990).

The groups of bilingual children were asked to choose one of the stories they had told during the course of the project and use it as the basis for a puppet show. These sessions were immensely popular with the children. Puppets were designed and made using a range of materials and techniques. One of the Sylheti groups spoke Sylheti throughout their complex discussions and negotiations with each other. The Malay group also spoke in their home language all the time. All the other bilingual groups again switched easily between English and their home language, with English once more being the dominant language overall. There was a noticeable difference in the languages preferred for different contexts: Year 6 children would largely speak in English to each other, but in home language when giving instructions or explanations to Y3 children. Y3 children were more likely to use home language in general than were Y6 children. The tendency to switch languages, and to mix languages within a sentence, were again evident both in groups speaking predominantly home language and groups speaking predominantly English. The switching (using languages alternately for different contexts) and mixing (using two languages within the same speech act) of languages in discussion and conversation suggests that these children are able to move freely between first and second language. Saima (Y6) explains:

> In school it depends who I am talking to like to the teachers or to Emma I will talk in English and to Saiqa I will talk in English because she usually talks in English but to Noreen or Shazma I will talk in both languages because they usually talk in both languages. When I am talking about maths, I will say half sentences in Mirpuri and half in English, or I will say half a paragraph in each language.

Saima clearly is not only aware of the language *she* prefers to use in a given context, but of the languages her peers prefer to use. She switches and mixes her languages accordingly. Saima has an assurance about her switching of languages, and is confident that she is equally competent in both English and her home language:

> I think I speak the best in both languages since in school I talk in English, at home I speak in both and at Mosque I speak in our language.

Romaine insists that switching and mixing of languages represents 'normal everyday instances of language use for the individuals concerned... yet for various reasons such instances of language use have been regarded both by linguists and laymen as somehow deviant and not ideal' (1989). In these children switching of languages according to the context seems to occur without conscious thought or deliberation. An important question emerges here: do bilingual children have an advantage in developing knowledge about language? Cummins and Swain (1986) provide a survey of recent research whose findings are consistent with Vygotsky's (1962) hypothesis that 'bilingualism can promote awareness of linguistic operations'. The switching and mixing of languages supports the notion that bilingual children become aware at an early age of the different uses and contexts of language:

> access to two languages in early childhood can promote children's metalinguistic awareness and possibly also broader aspects of cognitive development. (Cummins and Swain, 1986)

Nural, whose home language is Malay, uses Arabic at home for prayer before meals and at bedtime. She also tells of 'respectable words' and 'common words' in her language, which are dictated by their audience. Bodrul (Sylheti) suggested that there is a separate prefix in Sylheti depending whether one is speaking in a polite way, for example to a grandparent (in which case the prefix 'afni' is used), or a less formal way, for example to a child (in which case the prefix 'tui' is used). Bodrul insisted that these are rules which should never be broken. At a time when primary teachers are taking on National Curriculum targets in the teaching of knowledge about language, we would do well to make use of the existing resources of bilingual children.

Creating a positive multilingual classroom is not a simple matter of saying to children: 'You can speak the language you prefer'. Only by taking account of a variety of cultures in our curriculum planning will we provide real choice for children in their language use. Children will be encouraged to use their preferred language in the classroom (as they do naturally in other contexts) if we promote positive attitudes towards cultural diversity. If we want to create a successful multilingual classroom, the linguistic and cultural similarities and differences of the children should be central to their learning. In this way we can move towards the ideal of children feeling equally at ease in school with English and home language; then, like Saima, children may be able to say 'I think I speak the best in both languages'.

'Pakistani stories are really good stories'

When encouraged to use their home language for storytelling, bilingual children will bring to the classroom the narrative riches of their culture. Of the bilingual children telling stories in their home language as part of our project, the vast majority told a story which originated in their home culture. Of those bilingual children telling stories in English, fewer than half told a story which originated in their home culture. The majority of children working in English wrote stories drawn from experiences in their own domestic lives in Birmingham. In general, the stories originating in the home culture were more sophisticated then those of local origin. Shakila's story of 'The King and his Seven Wives', told in Mirpuri, was based in the rich narrative tradition of the Indian sub-continent; Saima's story, 'Three Wishes, No More!' was set in Pakistan, an adaptation of a tale she first heard in Mirpuri. She told the story in Mirpuri and wrote it in English. The children's stories originating in the home culture tended to have folk/fairy-tale characteristics, while stories set in local contexts tended to be more mundane accounts of daily life. Umar's Malaysian folk-tale of 'The Elephant and The Ants' provided a further example of a story told in home language, then written in English.

This apparent correlation between the use of home language and the telling of stories originating in the home culture provokes questions. If schools and local education authorities acknowledge the importance of teaching principles of co-operation, respect for each other and for other cultures, what is the place of languages in such a philosophy? Cummins (1986) makes the point that in order to value the languages and cultures of children in multilingual classrooms it is not necessary to actually teach in the minority language. This would be very difficult in a class where various children speak six or seven different languages. Teachers can, however, communicate to students and parents the extent to which the minority language and culture are valued by the school. By encouraging children to use their preferred languages at appropriate times in appropriate contexts teachers can build a bridge between the classroom and the culture of the community.

The following is part of a transcript of a conversation with two Mirpuri-speaking boys from the Year 6 group (these children, amazed that I could remember everyone's name after nine months out of their school, knew that I kept a photograph of the class on my desk):

T: Do you think you tell stories better in English or in Mirpuri?

Arfan: It isn't the language...

Atif: No, Sir it isn't...it isn't the language you say it in, it's just if the story's good, some stories are better than others, y'know, and

Arfan: some of our stories, y'know, Pakistani stories are really good stories and they go on for a really long time and they're not just for children they're for everyone, so we just remember them —

Atif: yes, Sir, it's like you remember our names from our photograph...we can just do it.

T: But are Pakistani stories better told in Mirpuri, or English or even Urdu?

Atif: No, Sir it doesn't matter, it's just that we have good stories and you can tell them in any language and they're the same.

This conversation provokes a further question: if we deny children access to their language and culture in the classroom, are we missing the opportunity to draw on a wealth of resources? Atif and Arfan were particularly animated and emphatic while making their points. Their argument that the quality of their narrative depends on the quality of the story, and that the best stories are those told as part of the Pakistani culture, is significant in planning for the classroom. If we are to make available the rich resources of the multilingual classroom, we must hand over to children some of the power to choose. If our aim is to empower bilingual children we must enable them to initiate curriculum change through their existing knowledge. In the active, child-centred classroom children write and publish their own books; if the books children publish are adaptations of stories originating in their culture, the teacher is not only sharing with them control of the curriculum, but genuinely valuing what the children have to offer. Savva (1990) points out that we should make *authentic* use of the linguistic diversity in our classrooms. Allowing children to develop real and meaningful work through their own language and culture contributes to an additive orientation; to pay lip-service to language and culture is to demean them, and contributes to subtractive bilingualism. Atif and Arfan quite clearly attach great value to the stories of their culture; if excellent work in the primary school relies on children's motivation and enthusiasm, then here is an opportunity too good to be missed. If the primary school is also about teaching and learning attitudes of co-operation, tolerance and respect for world cultures, then the stories of these children provide an invaluable resource. The active use of languages as a planned part of the usual curriculum will promote all children's understanding of cultural diversity; such an understanding can be enhanced in the multilingual primary classroom by making use of the stories children bring to school.

Conclusion

This chapter suggests an approach to curriculum planning and assessment in the primary school which actively and usually makes genuine use of children's languages to resource the primary classroom. Children and their families hold a wealth of learning opportunities. The stories they tell, which have perhaps never been written down before they write them; the chance to share part of their culture, and for that to be valued by other children; their knowledge of language use in different contexts; the opportunity to accord status to a variety of languages by making authentic use of them in the curriculum — all of these valuable resources are easily overlooked. If bilingual children are to use their whole linguistic repertoire in schools, they must be confident that their languages have a genuine role to play in all areas of the curriculum and in all areas of school life. Bilingual children switch between languages confidently and appropriately when encouraged; if we deny them this natural and usual facility we will inhibit their learning. An integrated approach to bilingual education will not simply provide a special topic on 'World Cultures' or 'Languages' every so often; it will put children's language and culture at the heart of their learning, and at the centre of teachers' curriculum planning. Only through a deliberate and committed bilingual education policy will we succeed in this aim. Unless they feel that their languages are regularly and normally accepted as an authentic medium for learning, children will speak English at school and their other languages at home. We must say loudly and clearly to bilingual children and their parents that English is not the only language of the school, and that the school values and respects the community in its planning and implementation of the curriculum. At the same time we must listen to the parents of bilingual children and work with them to develop bilingual education policy which teaches skills in English through the use of the full range of children's linguistic abilities. By these means schools will begin to provide an additive orientation to bilingual education, developing in children the ability, confidence and motivation to succeed.

Children's home languages are valuable as reinforcement of their cultural identity and as a source of learning opportunities. Languages cannot be ignored in a multicultural curriculum which focuses on respect for others, accords status to a variety of cultures and seeks to develop self-confidence, communication and collaboration. Children value their languages, and through them can bring to the classroom cultural strength and diversity. If we are serious about wanting to empower all children and provide full access to the curriculum, we must create an environment where children's whole linguistic and cultural experiences are an authentic and integral part of classroom life. In this way we will increase the confidence and achievement of bilingual children, and contribute to the development of all children's knowledge of, and respect for cultural diversity and equality.

References

Cummins, J. (1986) 'Empowering Minority Students: A Framework for Intervention' in *Harvard Educational Review* Vol. 56, No. 1.

Cummins, J. (1989) 'Language and Literacy Acquisition in Bilingual Contexts' in *Journal of Multicultural and Multilingual Development* Vol. 10 No. 3.

Cummins, J., and Swain, M. (1986) *Bilingualism in Education* Longman, Harlow.

Dodson, C.J. (1985) 'Second Language Acquisition and Bilingual Development: A Theoretical Framework' in *Journal of Multicultural and Multilingual Development* Vol. 6, No. 5.

Levine, J. (1990) *Bilingual Learners and the Mainstream Curriculum* Falmer, Lewes.

Romaine, S. (1989) *Bilingualism* Blackwell, Oxford.

Savva, H. (1990) 'The Rights of Bilingual Children' in Carter,R. (ed.) *Knowledge About Language and the Curriculum* Hodder and Stoughton, London.

Shan, S. (1990) 'Assessment by monolingual teachers of developing bilinguals at key Stage 1' in *Multicultural Teaching* Vol. 9 No. 1.

Tansley, P. (1986) *Community Language in Primary Education* NFER/Nelson, Windsor.

Chapter 4

Developing bilingual Theatre-in-Education programmes

Alison Reeves

Through bilingual Theatre-in-Education programmes a number of British companies aim to create an environment in which bilingual and monolingual pupils are able to enjoy a learning experience on equal terms. This chapter describes the developing practice of a Theatre-in-Education company in Birmingham as it set out to establish bilingual and bicultural practice in schools.

The use of bilingualism in the classroom is an important educational tool. The Cox Report (1989) followed in the footsteps of the Swann Report (1985) in stating that the emphasis in the primary classroom should be firmly on the development of a good command of English. At the same time the Cox Report asserted that 'the evidence shows that children will make greater progress in English if they know that their knowledge of their mother tongue is valued'. Arguments supporting the use of bilingualism in schools fall into three broad categories: educational, psychological and social. Trueba (1989) argues that 'emphasis should be shifted from English language development to general language development, so transference of cognitive skills and subject matter knowledge occurs between home language and English'. Trueba finds that cognitive development occurs through social interaction, and is inseparable from social development. Nixon (1985) suggests that language is closely linked to identity and a child's sense of self-worth:

the child's mother tongue is the means by which she gains a sense of herself as a sentient and responsible being, who is capable of communicating to members of a language community very different from her own and of acquiring the second language necessary to do so.

For all pupils the use of bilingualism in the classroom brings advantages of increased language and cultural awareness, which will increase communication between different cultural groups and so help to combat racism. The ethos of the school will gain from a truly multicultural approach which strengthens school and community links and sees the pupils' families as a resource.

My interest in the development of bilingual Theatre-in-Education programmes began after I visited India to work with the National School of Drama Theatre-in-Education Company in New Delhi. I returned keen to devise for *Language Alive!* Theatre-in-Education company in Birmingham a TIE programme about Indian Independence which would give status to these historical events. It was our aim that through working bilingually the cultural status of home and community languages would be raised, as would the cultural esteem of the pupils. The programme, *Azaad,* explores India's struggle for independence through the eyes of Meena, a young Indian woman. Pupils hear about Mahatma Gandhi's vision of a peaceful road to independence through the support of Meena's mother. Meena's friend Ranjit presents Bhagat Singh's radical, violent solution. Finally Meena's British teacher Mr. Bailey argues that although he believes India should be independent, independence should be achieved through constitutional means. Through empathising with the characters' experiences, pupils witness significant historical events. They are then asked to help Meena decide whether she should go on Gandhi's Salt March, a peaceful protest against the British salt laws and taxes. Teacher-actor Jaswinder Didially remained in the character of Meena, and spoke in Hindi and English. Then other teacher-actors played a range of British and Indian characters but only spoke in English. Bilingualism was incorporated into scenes so that sometimes a question asked in English would be answered in Hindi, but the conversation would be comprehensible in both languages.

We worked in secondary schools of very different cultural and linguistic character, ranging from Turves Green Boys School (95% White students) to Parkview School (95% Asian students) and Duddeston Manor School (an approximately equal mix of White, African Caribbean and Asian). I interviewed a group of pupils in each school immediately after they had seen the programme. I firstly asked the pupils how the programme made them feel about the British ruling in India. At Parkview two pupils related their sadness directly to the way 'English rules' had to be obeyed by the Indians and the way 'they were treated like servants'. One pupil related to Meena's situation in wanting to fight back 'even if you die'. A pupil at Duddeston Manor was able to universalise this feeling: 'it was like stealing something from another person.' When asked which characters they supported, most pupils in all three schools immediately sympathised with Meena and 'the decision she had to make.' In the same way most supported Meena's mother in her worry about whether her daughter would make 'the right decision or the wrong decision'. Significantly, a number of the Asian pupils agreed with Ranjit in her support of Bhagat Singh and 'the fact he was prepared to die for his country.' The condemnation of Mr. Bailey was unanimous in all three schools; many perceived him as one unable to sympathise with Indian independence because he was British and 'one of them.' Although the general level of awareness about the historical events in the programme was limited in all three schools, all of the pupils thought it was important 'to know about it, and how to handle it in case the same thing happens again.' A pupil at Turves Green Boys School personalised his response from a British perspective: 'Really we've got no right to rule their country.' None of the pupils felt that the use of Hindi as well as English prevented them from understanding the content. Some were perceptive about the way the languages were integrated in the programme, stating that Meena was 'answering and telling you what she was saying in her answer.' Pupils were positive about the use of Hindi, mainly because in the context of the programme it helped to contribute to the credibility of the Indian setting. Pupils in all three schools felt that characters other than Meena should have spoken in Hindi.

The fact that Asian pupils sympathised with Meena and recognised the significance of the historic events portrayed in the programme seemed to offer a confirmation that these pupils valued their own culture. The fact that White and African Caribbean students largely felt the same way suggested that we were meeting our objective of making all pupils aware of the value of another culture and language. Although the character of Meena presents a positive role model, there is a danger that presenting only one character using a community language can become a divisive strategy. In the past the Theatre-in-Education company's fear had been that they were deceiving pupils into believing that all company members spoke Asian languages fluently. However the support of pupils for other characters to speak bilingually in the programme encouraged each member of the company to speak some Hindi in the subsequent programme.

Kahaani was aimed at Year 2 (6-7 years) pupils, and was based on the traditional story of Moon Lake, as retold by Chand Ki Jeel. This provided an opportunity to develop traditional storytelling and song and dance techniques. The pupils were enrolled as animals who needed to protect their lake from the elephants, whose own lake had dried up. The programme was presented in two parts, allowing pupils to create dance movements which told aspects of the story. This was all framed in the context of two sisters preparing for the Monsoon celebrations. In our stated aims for the programme we included for the first time an explicit rationale for our use of bilingualism:

● To develop speaking and listening skills through storytelling

● To use traditional Indian music and dance forms to stimulate creative movement work

● To use bilingualism to enhance children's understanding and to promote the status of Asian languages

Our own and other companies' bilingual work in Theatre-in-Education was often tacked on to a very Eurocentric programme. The company was therefore keen to use Asian cultural forms in the programme. This was facilitated by local funding for two Asian musicians to work with us who were skilled in sitar and tabla. We used their expertise to select traditional songs and compose accompanying traditional music. We were also able to employ Chitraleka Bolar, a Bharatanatyam dancer, who taught us simple Indian dance movements. We also wanted to adopt the suggestion made by students during the *Azaad* programme that teacher-actors should use two languages. This meant that both teacher-actor Jaswinder Didially and I would speak some English and some Hindi in the programme. We also felt it was important that the programme had a modern context so that the pupils did not disregard the Asian culture as something historical and not living. While setting the programme firmly in Rajastan, we ensured that the programme made definite links with children's experience of life in Britain. We avoided setting the story in the context of a specific Muslim or Hindu festival, lest we alienate any particular group. Instead we chose a fictional festival to welcome the Monsoon rains, which had universal appeal and included information about the country. I again spoke to small groups of pupils from the three schools in Saltley to identify their response to the story and its bilingual presentation.

I was struck by the positive attitudes of bilingual and monolingual pupils to knowledge of more than one language. They clearly thought that it was an educational advantage to be bilingual, and that it was right and natural that I should speak some Hindi in the programme. One monolingual child felt that although he did not understand Hindi there was an opportunity here 'to learn other langauges'. The bilingual pupils were unanimous in their enthusiasm for the use of both languages, with responses ranging from bilingualism in school being 'fun' to their being able 'to learn a lot from it'. They made the same supportive response to my attempts at Hindi phrases, saying 'it is good because some English people don't speak Hindi', and 'I don't know Hindi but I can learn from other people.' The children felt that the action of the programme had helped their comprehension; they were very clear about the animal's movements: 'When you stamp your feet we know you are an elephant.' The children had followed the story visually, 'I saw the elephant went into the water and the moon was shaking because he was angry.' All were fascinated by the sitar, and listened avidly in silence. They visibly enjoyed singing the Hindi songs in the programme. Their enjoyment, and their entire lack of embarrassment, suggested that we were meeting our objective of raising the status of Indian culture through bilingual Theatre-in-Education.

At this point we wanted to rationalise our feeling that bilingual Theatre-in-Education was an appropriate strategy which can enable bilingual and monolingual children to enjoy a learning experience on equal terms. As part of this process we developed the following guidelines.

Bilingualism in Theatre-in-Education should be used to:

● Give status to children's languages and culture, enabling them to draw together the major influences of home, school and community.

● Support language learning of children who are not yet fluent in English by offering stories which are accessible to them. In this way they will increase awareness and understanding of language and cultural diversity for all pupils.

● Reflect a range of cultures in its programmes, including cultural forms which are not Eurocentric.

● Provide positive role models through all company members using both English and a community language in the programme.

● Present content visually, to provide contextual clues to understanding.

Voicebox, a new Theatre-in-Education company in Birmingham, developed bilingual work along these lines. *Voicebox* seeks not simply to use bilingualism as an educational tool, but to integrate two languages in the dramatic style of the piece for maximum theatrical impact. *Voicebox* began with *Familiar Feelings,* a programme written by Noel Greig for Year 1 and Year 2 (5-7 years) children. The central character is a five-year-old Asian girl called Kanta whose fifth birthday turns out to be a very strange day. Mr. Gradgrind arrives at her school with a test and Kanta finds that the right answers do not connect with her experiences at all. Searching for answers Kanta goes on a fantastic journey into the magic cupboard, where she discovers that there may be several answers to the same question. Jaswinder Didially provided a positive role model, playing the central character of Kanta; as she was the only Asian character in the play she was the only teacher-actor to speak Hindi. The artistic challenge was to add the Hindi lines without losing the simplicity of the script. The content was presented visually, with characters represented by large puppets (as big as the children watching the play), and the fantasy element of talking food was brought to life before their eyes.

The subsequent project *Cactus and Eagle* was devised for Years 4-6 (8-11 years) children; the programme explored the Spanish invasion of the Aztec city of Tenochtitlan, and its effect on one particular Aztec family.

The programme presented a new range of artistic problems; the company discussed whether it was appropriate to work bilingually in this case, as in reality none of the characters would have spoken either English or Hindi. In fact we were able to devise the bilingual script in a new way to show the lack of communication between the Spaniards and the Aztecs. The Aztec characters spoke in English and Hindi, while the Spaniards spoke only English. So now three of the company members were using community language as well as English in the play. On this occasion some of the children involved were Hindi speakers. Children watching and participating in the programme chatted freely in both languages and translated for their friends. The next programme, *Somewhere Safe*, was devised for Years 1 and 2 (5-7 years) children. This moved us on in our development of bilingual Theatre-in-Education. The starting-point was a monolingual script written by company member Hugh James. All company members used English, Panjabi and Sign Supported English in the programme. The content was made more accessible through the use of Sign Supported English and elements of British Sign Language, which visually echoed the spoken language of the play. We also tried to reflect the Asian culture in the content of the programme, integrating Asian dance gestures into the movement sections of the programme. Working in both Panjabi and English from the start of the planning process meant a more sophisticated use of the way the languages combine and compliment each other. Panjabi words were not simply chosen for what they added to the meaning of the story, but also for their poetic and rhythmic qualities.

Voicebox had moved from using bilateral bilingualism (i.e. one member of the company speaking Hindi and the others English) to full use of integrated bilingualism (in which all company members speak some Hindi and some English throughout). *Somewhere Safe* provided a focus for our *Equal Voices Festival,* Birmingham's first bilingual arts in education festival. The festival gave full recognition to the bilingual work of Theatre-in-Education companies, emphasising that bilingual work is essential to the needs of pupils in Birmingham schools. At the festival a group of teachers and non-teaching school staff joined us to explore ways in which bilingual and monolingual children can enjoy a learning experience on equal terms. Participants watched bilingual Theatre-in-Education programmes from *Voicebox, Neti-Neti* and *Half Moon Young People's*

Theatre. Workshops explored ways in which bilingual techniques can be used effectively, even when teachers themselves are monolingual.

Two important considerations for *Voicebox* were raised by the festival. In *Kola Pata Bhut (The Hopscotch Ghost)* by *Half Moon Young People's Theatre,* four actors moved easily between Sylheti, Bengali and English. The company had been able to devise, improvise and script their work in three languages, as more than one company member spoke Sylheti and Bengali fluently. Rather than taking a monolingual English script and translating it into other languages, *Half Moon YPT* was making authentic and genuine use of their community's linguistic resources. Secondly, the company was very much aware of the need to work from a bicultural perspective; it was not sufficient simply to add characters who spoke more than one language, as this was not addressing the needs of bicultural pupils in British schools. Consequently the company devised *Dear Suraiya...Love Rehana.* The play explores links between culture and commerce in Britain and Bangladesh, and is based on the central image of tea grown in Sylhet and consumed in Britain. The true story is told of Eklas Rehman, a union worker from Bangladesh who travelled to Britain to gain support for his members who work in poor conditions on British tea estates in Sylhet. This story is set against the fictional tale of two cousins, Rehana and Suraiya, one of whom lives in London, the other Bangladesh. Links between language and politics influenced the company's use of bilingualism, 'The relationship between a child's use of mother tongue and his/her educational development, the implication of language as a centre of resistance and the need to tackle the racism inherent in many received images of Bangladesh, formed the basis of our approach' (Bestwick, 1991). *Half Moon YPT* also felt that a bilingual programme would contribute to a sense of cultural identity; they wanted to go beyond positive role models and through the programme examine the dominant power of imperialism through a bilingual theatre form which in itself challenges dominant attitudes. In order to help dispel the myth that Bangladesh is an impoverished country propped up by British aid, the programme revealed how tea companies make more profit from tea than Britain gives in aid to Bangladesh. In this way the programme works relevantly and immediately within two cultures.

In *Voicebox's* programme *Meera Ka Savaal (The Child Who Challenged the King),* we have been able to directly tackle these two issues of biculturalism and the integration of two languages. We were able to employ a new company member, Seema Sethi, who spoke Hindi and Panjabi. This enabled Seema and Jaswinder to improvise and develop scenes in Hindi, and to add English at a later stage. This produced greater fluidity in the way languages were used in performance. Bicultural theatre was less straightforward to conceive. In order to raise the issue of children's rights we started with the true story of a fourteen-year-old girl who had been swopped at birth by mistake, and whose natural parents were now seeking custody. The girl had taken her natural parents to court to 'divorce' them. *Voicebox* initially set the story in contemporary India, but found that the story did not translate simply from its original American context. Instead the story was transposed to the court of King Akbar, whose role was to make judgement on the case. Pupils participated as court advisors, creating a Bill of Rights for the king to use as criteria in order to judge the case of the young girl. In this way the programme gave consideration to the cultural background and beliefs of the pupils. Once again we integrated Asian dance in the programme. The challenge for the future is to develop programmes which raise bicultural awareness without the need to distance the subject matter through a historical setting.

Theatre-in-Education is in a unique position to enable monolingual and bilingual pupils to enjoy a learning experience on equal terms. When talk is accompanied by movement, children and teachers who do not share a common home language can more easily share common meanings. Meaning can be transferred more easily between first and second language when both are used in parallel and are accompanied by visual clues. Theatre-in-Education encourages pupils to empathise with characters, to make sense of their experiences and to express their feelings. Bilingual Theatre-in-Education challenges the notion that if communication is to be of value it must be in English. The use of a range of languages in TIE programmes raises the status of those languages, and enhances the self-esteem of bilingual children. Bicultural TIE programmes enable pupils to develop the bicultural skills and awareness so vital for the success of bilingual children in British schools. Bestwick (1991) of *Half Moon YPT* captures childrens' response to bilingual Theatre-in-Education:

> The frisson of delight which skimmed through groups of Sylheti children when they first heard their language spoken on stage was unmistakable, while their English or monolingual classmates sur-

prised themselves that they could understand and enjoy a show partly in an unfamiliar language and gain confidence and interest in something which may have been a vaguely threatening unknown.

References

Bestwick, D. (1991) *Report on 'Dear Suraiya...Love Rehana'* Half Moon Young People's Theatre

Nixon, J. (1985) *A Teacher's Guide To Multicultural Education* Oxford, Basil Blackwell

Trueba, H. (1989) *Raising Silent Voices* New York, Newbury House Publications.

Chapter 5

The social process of a family literacy project with bilingual families

Martha Allexsaht-Snider

This chapter outlines a family literacy project for Spanish-speaking parents and children working together. I suggest that an understanding of the social process of literacy learning by these families can be applied to an examination of the assumptions and goals of family literacy programs in other bilingual and minority communities.

The research presented here views family reading activities in the context of broader family literacy activities. Rather than viewing reading as a literary or cognitive process, Bloome (1989) suggests that it should be seen as a social or cultural process. If we are to understand reading as a social process, we must consider what meanings are constructed in reading activities, how the broader socio-cultural context influences the construction of meaning, and what participants understand from participating in the activities (Green, 1990). Auerbach (1989) points out that although recent research on family literacy in minority communities (Delgado-Gaitan, 1987, 1990; Diaz, Moll & Mehan, 1986; Goldenberg & Gallimore, 1993; Trueba, 1984; Vasquez, 1991) has provided us with a broader definition that avoids the deficit model inherent in earlier studies, intervention programs do not yet reflect this new social-contextual approach to literacy. Family literacy research has framed a new perspective based on the assumptions that literacy learning must be seen in relation to its context and uses (Heath, 1983) and that it also needs to acknowledge the families' social realities and help them to act on them (Freire, 1970). The Carpinteria family literacy program was designed to close the gap between what has been learned from the ethnographic literature on family contributions to literacy and what is happening in the implementation of family literacy programs (Auerbach, 1989). In the following pages I apply frameworks for understanding reading and literacy as social processes to the analysis of the parents' experiences in the project's workshops and parent-child reading activities in the home.

The Family Literacy Project

The Family Literacy Project began when ten sets of Spanish-speaking parents (husbands and wives except in the case of one single parent) accepted an invitation to attend a program of eight monthly meetings as an offshoot of Delgado-Gaitan's (1990) research on family-school linkages in the community of Carpinteria. At each meeting parents were issued a children's literature book in Spanish that served as the basis of a workshop led by another parent and the researchers. The workshop focused on strategies adults could use during reading with their children. Prior to beginning the program, parents were interviewed about the literacy practices and environment in the home. They were videotaped reading with their children at this time. Videotaping was done three times during the program, and again about eight months later. At the time of the latter follow-up video, they were also interviewed about the project.

The initial interviews with the families yielded data regarding the family schooling backgrounds, home literacy environments, and family literacy practices that informed the planning for the organisation and content of the Family Literacy Project intervention. The interviews confirmed the findings of Chall and Snow (1982), Delgado-Gaitan (1990), Goldenberg and Gallimore (1993), Taylor and Dorsey-Gaines (1988), and Trueba (1984), that a range of literacy practices and materials were found in the homes of working-class, minority, and language minority families.

This finding is in contrast to the assumption often made by social scientists that these homes are 'literacy impoverished.'

Families who participated in the project shared several characteristics. They were immigrants from México, working class, and predominantly Spanish-speaking. Their schooling and literacy backgrounds varied considerably, however, and subsequently their social, linguistic, and contextual presuppositions about what is required to participate in reading activities (Gumperz, 1986) also varied. The Alvarez and Rios family exemplify this range. Mr. Alvarez had completed sixth grade in México and had attended high school in the United States where he had learned to speak and read English, while his wife had only completed sixth grade in México. They both read newspapers, magazines and books at home in Spanish. Mr. Alvarez also read newspapers in English. In contrast, the Rios family spoke Nahuatl as their first language and Spanish as a second language. Neither parent could read or write, so their older children eased matters by reading for them.

The information from initial interviews about parents' diverse experiences with literacy and varied experiences in reading with their children was used in planning a program with a flexible organisational structure that built on family strengths, fostered interaction between parents, and made reading a social activity. The requirements for participation in the project were defined as broadly as possible. Parents' and children's oral literacy skills were acknowledged and given value through the interviews and in workshops. The parents were encouraged to view oral interpretation of text as a skill independent of ability to decode print (Hale, 1980). Since many parents reported that one parent was more literate than the other, joint or group interpretation of text was practiced in the workshop and home settings so that participation in literacy activities was not limited by parents' or children's relative lack of decoding skills. Joint participation meant that they could build on each other's knowledge. Both parents (and in one case an older son) in each family were encouraged to participate in the program.

The understandings of home literacy contexts that emerged from the initial interviews were integrated with the social-contextual approach of family literacy advocated by Auerbach and implemented by Ada (1988), Freire (1970) and others. The training was built on parents' knowledge and experience by encouraging them to discuss with their children how to apply their own life experiences to find meaning in the text. The monthly workshop sessions on reading with children were introduced with a brief presentation of a new book by a parent leader in which he or she read part of the book and asked questions to stimulate discussion about the text in relation to the families' experiences (for discussion of a similar program see Ada, 1988). The introduction was followed by small group sessions in which parents took turns reading aloud from the text and posed questions for each other to draw out the relationship between the text and their own experiences. Those who were more experienced in interacting with text took the lead, while parents who were less confident in their skills learned from the joint reading activities with other parents. The workshops were organised in a monthly series so that the understandings developed in the workshop settings could be enacted in reading activities at home. Parent-child reading activities at home were followed by meetings where parents could raise questions and concerns, thereby reconstructing the reading activity with their children on an ongoing basis and also collaborating in a critical examination of their roles in shaping their children's education (Delgado-Gaitan, 1992).

Reading as a Social Process

If reading is viewed as a social or cultural process, then the Family Literacy Project can be said to reveal several views of the reading process. The meanings attached to reading during the project can be seen to have been constructed in parent-child, parent-parent, and researcher-parent interactions. Parents had initially attached meaning to the reading activity with their children based on their past schooling experiences in either México or the United States, or on whether they were readers or non-readers. Parents held diverse views of what counted as literacy, what kinds of resources they had to apply in literacy activities, and whether or not they had access to literacy (Taylor, 1981; Szwerd, 1988).

A new, shared framework for the reading activities (Weade & Green, 1989) was negotiated by the parents, parent leaders, and researchers during the workshops. Parents had initially reported reading aloud only with their younger children who could not yet read on their own. Over the months of the project, as parents read aloud together and discussed the books they later read with their children, they saw that they could participate with their older children in jointly understanding text. The parents continued to share reading at home with the older children. One of the later videotapes showed, for example, a father and daughter talking about a school literature book, *Isla de los Delfines Azules* (Island of the Blue Dolphins) that they had been enjoying together. The father pointed out the locations in the text that were in the vicinity and which they had visited.

Parents who initially saw the purpose of joint reading activities as improving their children's decoding skills and fluency in reading aloud, found through participating in reading with their children that another more encompassing purpose was to make reading activities at home meaningful and enjoyable for the children. Table 1 (page 77) illustrates the meanings held by the participants in the study in the nine months of the project. In the following paragraphs, I discuss two family cases to show the social process of reading and literacy activities for families in the project.

Family Case Studies

Mrs. Macías read regularly with Alicia and encouraged her to read the newspaper because she thought it was important for her daughter to know what was going on in the world. At night when she read with her daughter, Mrs. Macías asked Alicia questions to try to make sure that she was understanding. Mrs. Macías thought Alicia was not doing well in reading because she could not explain what she was reading. Alicia's mother was actively involved with homework and other literacy activities associated with her daughter's schooling. She read in both Spanish and English. Unlike some other parents, she did not express a frustration about not being able to help Alicia with her reading and homework due to her own lack of schooling and reading. Instead, she was concerned with Alicia's lack of independence and unwillingness to read and do homework on her own.

The Soto family also had a daughter, Estrella, who was the oldest of three children. Mr. Soto attended secondary school in México, and his wife attended only a few years of primary school. Mrs. Soto had learned to speak English through her work, and had developed some reading and writing skills in English. There were books, magazines and newspapers in the home, and the family visited the local library regularly. Mrs. Soto thought that Estrella was a good reader, that she had a very open mind.

The mother thought they, especially her husband, needed to pay more attention to their daughter. Mrs. Soto added,

Que él sabe leer más mejor que yo. Ayudarle a ella quizá está leyendo así en voz alta él necesita decirle 'Así se hace'. Por que él tuvo más estudio que yo ¿verdad? Yo le puedo leer pero no sé ni donde están las puntuaciones. [He knows how to read better than I do. To help her when she's reading out loud he needs to tell her 'This is how you do it'. Because he studied more than I did, you know? I can read, but I don't know where to put the punctuation].

The parents in these two cases began the project with similar backgrounds in literacy and similar understandings of the reading activities with their children, although there were distinct differences, too. In both families, at least one parent had Spanish literacy skills at approximately a sixth grade level and those parents were confident about applying their own reading skills in assisting their children. Both families initially saw the purpose of reading as finding information or gaining knowledge or wisdom. The two sets of parents differed in their goals for reading with their children, however. Mrs. Macías was concerned about her daughter developing independence in reading and doing her homework. Mr. and Mrs. Soto focused on the need to develop Estrella's pronunciation and use of pauses and intonation in reading aloud a passage in a meaningful way. A second difference in the two families was that Mrs. Soto, in contrast to Mrs. Macías, saw herself as lacking literacy skills in Spanish and therefore less able to assist her daughter with schoolwork.

The patterns of interaction in the videotaped reading sessions were similar in the two families. Both parents initiated little or no discussion with the girls in the first observations. In both cases, the girls responded reluctantly, vaguely, and briefly to their parents' efforts to question them about their reading. For example, Mrs. Macías asked, «¿Cuál es el título?» (What is the title?) and Alicia answered, 'A gozar en casa' (Having a good time at home). When her mother tried to relate the title to Alicia's experience by asking, '¿Qué es para ti gozar en casa? (What does it mean for you to have a good time at home?), Alicia responded vaguely, 'Hacer una cosa.' (Doing something). In the second session, Mrs. Soto asked, '¿Ese es el papá?' (Is this the father?) and Estrella responded, 'No.' Her

TABLE 1: The Social Process of Reading Activities in The Family Literacy Project

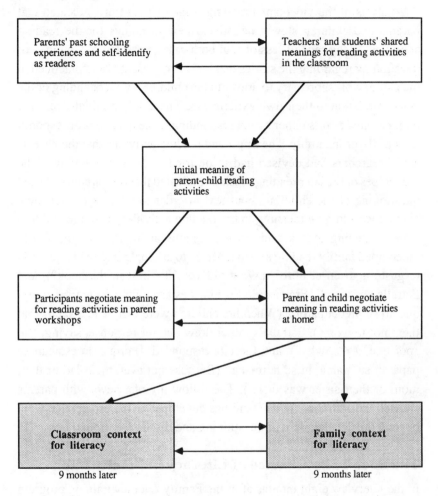

mother continued, '¿Quíen es este señor? (Who is this man?) and Estrella answers, 'Un señor.' (A man.)

Analysis of the videotaped reading sessions over time indicated that parents and children slowly negotiated new meanings for the reading activities. In the second sessions, in both cases, parents used the idea of questioning regarding the stories that had been presented and practiced in the parent workshop to try to draw out the children's understanding of the story in relation to their own experiences. The children initially resisted their parents' efforts either by not responding to the questions or responding briefly or inaudibly. The improved reading activities that the parents and researchers had devised had to be tried in the home settings. The videotapes of the later reading sessions indicated that the parents had used questioning of the children about text in order to relate it to their own experiences, to give meaning to the reading activities; also, the children were beginning to ask their own questions abput text. In the fourth videotaped family reading session, Mr. Soto asked, '¿Qué fué lo que más te gustó aquí en el libro?' (What did you like best in the book?), and Estrella answered, 'Era cuando los niños estaban ahí y un marinero dijo que no se preocuparon.' (When the children were there and a sailor told them not to worry). Estrella's father drew out her response, saying, 'Sí, ¿por qué? (Yes, why?), and Estrella responded, 'Porque no estaban su papá, ni su mamá, ni su hermana.' (Because not even their dad or their mom or their sister was there.). The follow-up interviews with parents showed the additional understandings developed in the project that went beyond the development of questioning and discussion around text.

The Social Significance of Literacy in Family Life

In the interview eight months after the Family Literacy training program ended, Mrs. Macías found the program useful because

> He podido tener más comunicación con [mi hija]. [La comunicación he mejorado] en estar más unidos y de comprenderlos tambien a ellos. [I've been able to have more communication with [my daughter]. [The communication has gotten better in that] we are more united and understand each other better.]

Mr. Soto echoed the same theme of family unity emerging from participation in the project, as did many of the other parents. In his words, 'Este proyecto ayudó mucho a la unión familiar.' (This project helped a lot with family unity.) Mrs. Macías also indicated that she had learned from getting together with other parents that she wasn't the only one who had concerns about her daughter's lack of independence and motivation in reading. The discussions with other parents had helped her not to feel inhibited about participating in her daughter's schooling. She summarised, saying

> Tenemos que quitarnos esa pared que nos dividide de decir el hijo va a la escuela, en la escuela aprende todo y yo ya no tengo nada que ver. Y eso no es cierto. [We need to break down the wall that divides us, where we say that my child goes to school, she learns everything in school and I don't have anything to do with it. That's not true.]

Mr. Soto noted that his participation in reading activities with Estrella had affected the other children in the family as well, 'ahora mis hijos los más pequeños tambien quieren leer.' (Now my other younger children also want to read.). Mrs. Soto added that she thought the project had helped the children, but it had also helped her. She felt it was very helpful for parents who had not had much schooling because they read more and understood better what they were reading.

The two cases presented here illustrate the different starting points in terms of literacy backgrounds, home literacy environments, and goals for the parent-child reading activities for the Macías and Soto families. While the social processes of the reading activities in the home and the workshops were experienced in similar ways in the two families, they reported different changes in self-perception, relations of family members, and involvement in school-related activities (Cochran, 1988). Auerbach (1989) asserts that 'The goal of a social-cultural approach to family literacy is to increase the social significance of literacy in family life by incorporating community cultural forms and social issues in the content of literacy activities' (p. 177). The research discussed here suggests that an approach that incorporates families' native languages, community cultural forms and social issues, as well as reading as a social process, can fit families' goals for becoming literate.

The experiences of the parents and children in the Carpinteria Family Literacy Project confirm an assertion made by Auerbach (1989) in summarising the implications of a social-contextual model for family literacy. The family literacy model, as such, is not a pre-determined curriculum or set of practices or activities. Instead, the model implies a set of questions to be asked about the context for family literacy programs in a particular community that can be used to guide program planning. The following are some suggested guiding questions: (1) What are the meanings that parents and children attach to literacy activities, and what are their goals for these activities? (2) What is the context for literacy learning in the family, community, and school settings? (3) How does the organisational and social structure of a family literacy program support or constrain the families' participation in reading and literacy learning activities? (4) In what ways does the program support or constrain parents in shaping their and their children's social contexts?

References

Ada, A. F. (1988). The Pajaro Valley experience: Working with Spanish-speaking parents to develop children's reading and writing skills in the home through the use of children's literature. In T. Skutnabb-Kangas, & J. Cummins (Eds.), *Minority Education: From shame to struggle*. Philadelphia: Multilingual Matters.

Allexsaht-Snider, M. (1989). *Language, culture, and schooling: Family literacy project at Morgan Elementary School.* Unpublished manuscript University of California, Graduate School of Education, Santa Barbara.

Auerbach, E. (1989). Toward a social-contextual approach to family literacy. *Harvard Educational Review, 59*(2), 165-181.

Bloom, D. (1989). Locating the learning of reading and writing in classrooms: Beyond deficit, difference, and effectiveness models. In C. Emihovich (Ed.), *Locating learning: Ethnographic perspectives on classroom research* (pp. 87-114). Norwood, NJ: Ablex.

Chall, J. S., & Snow, C. (1982). *Families and literacy: The contributions of out of school experiences to children's acquisition of literacy.* A final report to the National Institute of Education.

Cochran, M. (1988). Between cause and effect: The ecology of program impacts. In A.R. Pence (Ed.), *The social construction of literacy.* New York: Cambridge University Press.

Cook-Gumperz, J. (1986). Introduction: the social construction of literacy. In J. Cook-Gumperz (Ed.), *The social construction of literacy.* New York: Cambridge University Press.

Delgado-Gaitan, C. (1987). Parent perceptions of school: Supportive environments for children. In H. Trueba (Ed.), *The social construction of literacy.* New York: Cambridge University Press.

Delgado-Gaitan, C. (1990). *Literacy for empowerment: The role of parents in children's education.* London: Falmer Press.

Delgado-Gaitan, C. (1992). Sociocultural change through literacy: Toward the empowerment of families. In B. Ferdman, R. M. Weber, & A. Ramirez (Eds.), *Literacy across languages and cultures*. New York: SUNY Press.

Delgado-Gaitan, C., & Allexsaht-Snider, M. (1990, April). *Family literacy project*. Research report presented at the annual meeting of the Linguistic Minority Research Project, University of California, Santa Cruz.

Diaz, S., Moll, L., & Mehan, H. (1986). Socio-cultural resources in instruction: A context-specific approach. *Beyond Language: Social and cultural factors in schooling language minority children*. Los Angeles: California State Department of Education and California State University.

Freire, P. (1970). *Pedagogy for the oppressed*. New York: Seabury Press.

Goldenberg, C. (1987). Low-Income Hispanic Parents' Contributions to their First-Grade Children's Word-Recognition Skills. *Anthropology and Education Quarterly, 18*(3), 149-179.

Goldenberg, C., & Gallimore, R. (1991). Local Knowledge, Research Knowledge, and Educational Change: A Case Study of Early Spanish Reading Improvement. *Educational Researcher, 20*(8), 2-14.

Green, J. L. (1990). *Reading is a social process*. In the Proceedings of the Australian Reading Association annual conference. Canberra: Australian Reading Association.

Gumperz, J. J. (1986). Interactional sociolinguistics in the study of schooling. In J. Cook-Gumperz (Ed.), *The social construction of literacy*. New York: Cambridge University Press.

Hale, A. (1980). The social relationships implicit in approaches to reading. *Reading, 14*(2), 24-30.

Heath, S. B. (1983). *Ways with words*. Cambridge, U.K.: Cambridge University Press.

Szwerd, J. F. (1988). The ethnography of literacy. In E. P. Kintgen, B. M. Kroll, & M. Rose (Ed.), *Perspectives on literacy*. Carbondale, IL: Southern Illinois University.

Taylor, D. (1982). Family literacy: The social context of learning to read and write.(Doctoral dissertation, Teachers College, Columbia University, (1981). *Dissertation Abstracts International, 41*, 12A.

Taylor, D., & Dorsey-Gaines, C. (1988). *Growing up literate: Learning from inner-city families*. Portsmouth, NH: Heineman.

Trueba, H. (1984). The forms, functions, and values of literacy: Reading for survival in a barrio as a student. *NABE Journal, 9*(11), 21-40.

Vasquez, O. A. (1991). Reading the world in a multicultural setting: A Mexicano perspective. *The Quarterly Newsletter of the Laboratory of Comparative Human Cognition, 13*(1), 13-15.

Weade, R., & Green, J. (1989). Locating reading. In C. Emihovich (Ed.), *Locating learning: Ethnographic perspectives on classroom research*. Norwood, NJ: Ablex.

Chapter 6

Integrating ESL into the mainstream: an Australian perspective

Chris Davidson

Introduction

It seems a foolhardy task to offer a national perspective on an issue as complex as English as a Second Language (ESL) teaching in a country as diverse as Australia. Australia is a federation of states and territories with constitutional responsibility for schooling in the compulsory years, yet there is now an established tradition of federal intervention in, and substantial indirect funding of, English as a Second Language (ESL) programs in schools. There are three large autonomous school systems; State, Catholic and private, and education is divided into two distinct sectors, primary and post-primary. Within some state systems there are also semi-autonomous intensive language centres which have historically catered for recently arrived children from a language background other than English in their first six to twelve months in Australia.

Many ESL children arrive in Australian schools speaking very little or no English. They may be the children of refugees, migrants, or business people. Their first language may be a well-developed standard variety or it may be a mixed, almost pidginized variety of their parents' mother tongue and English, picked up from siblings and peers. They may have started school in their country of origin, or have severely-interrupted or no schooling prior to entering the Australian education system. If they were born in Australia they are more likely to begin literacy in English.

Despite this diversity in learner profile and program delivery, a common philosophical base and common goals have emerged in Australian school ESL programs over the last twenty or so years. A relatively favourable political, economic and social climate has led to the development of some policies and practices which are in the forefront of multicultural education world-wide. One of the most significant of these developments is the 'mainstreaming' of ESL provision. This article seeks to analyse this movement, especially the ways in which it is has changed and then to highlight the challenges that mainstreaming still poses for students, teachers and policy makers in Australia today.

Snapshots — From then 'til now.

A Brisbane migrant reception centre, 1954.

An English class for New Australians.....'The red book is bigger than the blue book. Repeat after me'. School-age children play outside in the dusty heat, shouting excitedly in a multitude of different tongues, while educational authorities prepare to pass judgement on their capacity to 'pick-up' English, as if by osmosis.

A Sydney inner suburban high school, 1973

A muddy football oval, flanked by a cluster of drab brown demountable buildings, supplied courtesy of the Federal Government of Australia. Within the nearest, like its neighbours defaced by graffiti, a class is underway. Its teacher officially the 'migrant English teacher', although she does not feel worthy of the title. She has had only a five day inservice, including a foreign language demonstration lesson, and a free gift of adult teaching materials, the ubiquitous Situational English, to prepare her for her role. She has resigned from her job with the state education system to become a temporary employee of the Federal Government's recently established Child Migrant Education Program (CMEP). Her contact with the other staff of the school is minimal, but her students are even more isolated from their peers. In the closest school building, a predominantly

Anglo-Australian class of thirteen-year-olds is doing a project on Captain Cook, 'the first man to discover Australia', but the content of the 'migrant English' syllabus is grammatical structures and pronunciation drills with little or no modification for the needs of children. After a few months of English language assistance, these children, mostly southern European, will be shunted across the muddy divide to be 'assimilated' into the host school. Many will not make it, but jobs are plentiful and expectations are low.

A Melbourne primary school, 1987

A lively, noisy classroom of children from many different language backgrounds ...one of a number of open-plan spaces in a double-storey, modern, red-brick building. Bright pictures crowd the walls, jostling for space with the slogans and checklists surrounding displays of childrens' 'stories' in many different languages. All children are 'immersed' in language, 'actively engaged' in learning, involved at every turn in 'purposeful communication' and provided with a 'rich learning environment'. The philosophy is 'learner-centred','self-directed', 'process-oriented', 'whole language'. The teachers appear competent, aware, totally professional, working in teams with flexible and multi-level groupings of students. Yet there are discordant notes...an uncomprehending smile here, a behavioural problem there, a slightly frenetic note to the endless stream of teacher talk and constant change of activities. Where is the ESL teacher, you ask? All our teachers are ESL teachers, the principal replies.

An Adelaide outer metropolitan K-12 college, 1993

School has finished for the day...a large group of teachers are sitting around a whiteboard in an empty classroom, take away pizza on the table. ....An *ESL in the Mainstream* inservice is underway. Science, Maths and Social Studies teachers enthusiastically debate the ways to adapt a Science textbook for a multi-ethnic class. The ESL teacher recommends shredding it and they laugh. They use linguistic terminology very comfortably and seem to be in no hurry to finish the discussion. The ESL teacher, also the Senior School Co-ordinator, asks her colleagues to explain some concepts that she didn't understand in the senior Physics class she co-teaches. This leads to a discussion about general student needs and another teacher suggests the school language policy be revised to include guidance for teachers on textbook selection...The Principal joins the group and recommends raising the matter at the next meeting of the school Curriculum Committee.

From the margins to the mainstream

The development of child ESL programs in Australia can be seen as an unsteady but gradually accelerating movement from the margins of school life into the often muddy and treacherous waters of the mainstream.

It is a source of national embarrassment to the education profession in Australia that prior to the 1970s, the need for English language assistance for the children of migrants was never officially acknowledged. Although the national Adult Migrant Education Program had been established in 1947, the attitude of the state school sector at the time is exemplified by a comment from the Secretary, Education Department of Victoria to the General Secretary of the Victorian Teachers Union in October, 1954, quoted in Martin (1985:2)

> If these children are given some attention by the class teacher, they cause no serious problem

Where migrant children were considered a 'problem', that problem was individual-psychological, never structural. Such children were branded as having learning difficulties, although the South Australian Haines Report (SA Department of Education 1956:2) observed that it was diffi-cult 'to make a really accurate check of these children' as headmasters differ on what constitutes backwardness'. Needless to say, there was no recognition of these students as a group with distinct and unmet needs, and ESL programs, even in the most assimilationist form, did not exist.

After many years of lobbying, a Child Migrant Education Program (CMEP) was finally established in 1971. It was a Federal Government initiative, a short-term measure to employ teachers to teach newly-arrived migrant children English, giving them in-service training. It was envis-aged that once the 'backlog of remedial work' with children already in the educational system was handled, there would be few demands on the program. The program itself was based on the prevailing philosophy of 'change the child — by teaching him English — and no other change would be needed' (Martin 1978:113)

These initial assumptions about the purpose and scope of the CMEP influenced both the nature of the program offered and the role of the 'migrant English teacher'. The curriculum and resources developed by the Federal Government bore little or no relationship to the goals and content of the school programs, being derived from adult English language learning materials, based on decontexualised grammatical structures and drill and practice exercises. Teachers were employed directly by the Federal Government and had little or no contact with staff of the host school. According to Martin (1978:118),

> They were marginal to schools and to the teaching profession and had little incentive to see their function in anything but the narrowest technological terms. Their status was generally low and their voices not heard in high places.

However, this was a turning point in the development of the ESL field. The late seventies and early eighties gradually ushered in a period of marked change in the conceptualisation of the ESL learner and, as a consequence, a dramatic shift in the role and content of the ESL program, especially in its relationship to the mainstream.

TESOL was acknowledged as a permanent and integral component of educational and settlement services. Professional TESOL associations and ethnic communities were established, first locally, then rapidly expanding in size and influence. Teacher training courses were set up and materials development workshops proliferated.

In the political arena a number of policy documents were being formulated that would be international firsts in language and multicultural education, including the very influential National Policy on Languages (Lo Bianco 1987).

Whole school approaches to ESL became the catch-cry and the barriers between TESOL and the rest of the education world came tumbling down. The relationship between ESL and the mainstream was turned upside down. In the words of Campbell and McMeniman (1985:32):

> The path ahead lies in reconceptualising so-called 'mainstream' programmes so that they cater adequately for the needs of the total population. It should not be a question of 'NESB (Non-English-speaking Background) versus the Rest', but of acknowledging that, having been bought into Australia, NESB persons are now 'us'.

Rhetoric, however, far outstripped reality. Mainstreaming became a double-edged sword, seized upon by some sections of the community as an excuse to abandon all affirmative-action and ethnic-specific programs, from ethnic broadcasting through to direct ESL instruction in schools. The number of TESOL specialists in schools declined, ESL programs in a number of states were savagely cut. In Victoria official policy on mainstreaming was interpreted as forbidding the segregation of students with similar language needs for any purposes. The distinctions between ESL and the mainstream, once a yawning chasm, were blurred and collapsed. Mainstreaming began to be seen by many as a return to assimilation in another guise.

By the late eighties, however, educators had begun to fight back, publicly branding 'mainstreaming' for the Trojan Horse it was. There was a groundswell of concern to conceptualise and communicate what was distinctive about the ESL learner as well as what was shared with Anglo-Australian peers. The notion that the 'mainstream' itself was some monolithic identity was challenged and discredited.

The conceptualisation of ESL and the mainstream

The current conceptualisation of the relationship between ESL and the mainstream in Australia can perhaps best be captured by looking first at the learner, then at the program and the teacher.

It has been argued (Davison 1990) that the ESL learner has needs which are both similar to, yet also very different from, the 'mainstream' child. Both groups are very diverse but certain generalisations can be made about their cultural, linguistic and learning needs.

For the ESL learner, cultural needs are two-fold, encompassing both the need for more explicit information about, and induction into the Anglo-Australian culture, values, and socio-political processes, and the need to have the students' own ethnolinguistic and sociocultural background supported and explicitly recognised by the broader school community. The curriculum must help to confirm and legitimate the children's cultural experiences and understandings and, at the same time, challenge and extend them. The Anglo-Australian peer culture is also very different from the school culture, but there is a much greater gap between the norms and values of the Anglo-Australian community and those of the ESL child. This difference tends to be underestimated, even by the most sensitive and aware teachers. The school needs to bridge this gap and not rely on students to make the connections. Obviously, effective home-school liaison is particularly important as is the provision of multilingual materials and interpreters.

The language needs of ESL children are both more subtle and yet more obvious than their cultural needs. Language is very much a product of the cultural conventions and assumptions of the society from which it springs. For example, the Anglo-Australian concern with relevance and directness is manifested in a very linear style of discourse and, to many NESB groups, little subtlety in choice of vocabulary. These differences between language forms mean that ESL children are generally ahead of their peers in one sense, yet behind them in another. Unlike the vast majority of Anglo-Australian children, ESL students have the advantage of bilingual-ism. They come to the learning of English as fluent users of the language they grew up speaking. They know that spoken language is purposeful. They know how to combine a large range of sounds and gestures into meaningful units in order to communicate. They have had years of practice in interpreting quite subtle nuances in their mother tongue. With skilful encouragement, they will bring what they already know about language learning and language use to the second language learning task. Their bilingualism, especially if maintained and developed, will give them greater cognitive and linguistic flexibility. Bilingualism also appears to promote a better understanding of how language in general operates and this knowledge, if shared in the mainstream classroom, will help raise all children's awareness of language.

On the other hand, it is obvious that ESL children are also disadvant-aged to the extent that their first language is not the language of the school nor the medium of teaching, nor, in most cases, an object of instruction. Thus, ESL learners have to acquire a whole new sound system, a new set of words and meanings, a new way of constructing sentences and a new set of discourse patterns. They must learn to express themselves clearly in a language that is appropriate for their age, their situation and their purpose. Unlike their Anglo-Australian peers, ESL learners do not have a sound oral base in English upon which to build their literacy skills and there are likely to be many gaps in their knowledge.

At the same time as they are coming to grips with English, they are expected to be learning a range of new concepts and skills without the support of the mother-tongue (Cleland & Evans 1986). ESL students cannot be expected to pick up language by osmosis — they need an explicit and planned language program integrated with their general classwork that takes into account their specialised needs and different stages of development. They also need on-going maintenance and development of their mother-tongue, preferably through some form of bilingual program.

The learning needs of ESL children are both similar to and different from the needs of their Anglo-Australian peers. The *processes* underlying first and second language acquisition appear to be basically the same, thus all children in the class will benefit from a language-rich, relaxed environment, and from involvement in activities that give them many opportunities to use language successfully, to interact with others, and to communicate in a range of contexts. However, because ESL children are coming to the learning of English at a much later stage of cognitive and linguistic development and because they have much less exposure to English, they have certain specialised needs. In terms of classroom procedures, they need much more repetition and practice, more explicit instruction and concept-checking, more careful paraphrasing of vocabulary, more demonstration and modelling, more highly structured and sensitive elicitation of existing knowledge, more opportunities for controlled teacher-student and student-student interaction and more time to absorb the rhythms and patterns of the target language. They need methodical, planned language *development,* not just opportunities for use.

In addition, ESL children often have very different expectations of the teaching/learning process, particularly if they have done some schooling in their country of origin. They may be reluctant, for example, to question an adult teacher or to participate in group discussions, as these are not appropriate forms of behaviour for a child in their own cultural group. They may also suffer from cultural disorientation and their self-esteem may have been undermined by their initially dependent, even infantilized status. Such children will need more reassurance and support with their learning than their Anglo-Australian peers. Teachers need to make the purpose of classroom activities more explicit and provide opportunities for such children to share their anxieties or reservations with bilingual support staff or children who speak the same first language.

At some stage in their development, almost all ESL learners will benefit from regular and intensive small group work with a qualified and experienced ESL specialist. This may be through an introductory period in an intensive language centre integrated into a school, or it may be through time-tabled parallel or elective classes or through flexible groupings within the mainstream classroom.

The majority of long-term resident or Australian-born ESL children, particularly in the early years of primary school can be catered for within the mainstream, provided that the content and methodology is adapted. Their needs cannot be met by immersion alone, no matter how stimulating the activities (Kay 1990, Gibbons 1991). ESL learners must have a carefully integrated program of both language-conscious content teaching **and** content-based language instruction.

What does such a program look like? In what way is it similar to or different from a normal Australian primary classroom?

In Australia, most primary teachers have been very influenced by whole language and natural learning approaches (Cambourne 1988). 'Natural learning' is based upon the way young children appear to acquire oral language very easily and naturally when exposed continually to other speakers of the language using it in a meaningful context.

As a classroom teacher explains (Ministry of Education, Victoria, 1988):

> By experimenting with language and refining their use of it in the light of feedback they receive, children learn how to make language work for them. Writing and reading are natural extensions of this — further ways of communicating information for all kinds of purposes. Not only are the children immersed in oral language, they are surrounded by a stimulating print environment, ranging from labels and game instructions to literature and their own 'published' stories

The natural learning approach supplies a very rich and, potentially very rewarding atmosphere for the language development of ESL students.

It is now accepted wisdom that the ESL child will learn faster if the language is purposeful and whole in the sense that it conveys meaning, and especially if it arises from concrete activities where visual clues prompt understanding. And if able speakers of English join in these activities and provide a language model that can be copied, then the ESL learner's progress is likely to be enhanced.

However, most whole language programs that follow the principles of natural learning need a bit of patching in order to cater effectively for *all* students. Look at the following extracts from two authentic work programs for Year 2 children. One comes from an outer suburban primary school with virtually no ESL students, the other from an inner-city school with an enormously diverse mix of ethnic groups. Which is the ESL-modified program?

WORK PROGRAM: *Extract 1*

Topic: Cleanliness/Hygiene

☐ Discussion of ways of keeping clean

☐ Visit from dentist/doctor

☐ Ways of brushing your teeth

☐ Survey of how many times a day we brush our teeth

☐ Sleep time — Graph of hours

☐ Ways of cleaning clothes

☐ Types of clothes we can wear

☐ Project on clothes

☐ Research on the roles of people who look after us e.g. Dentist, Doctor

☐ Excursion to the dentist's and doctor's

☐ Survey Questions about what to ask a dentist/doctor about his job

☐ If I were a dentist

☐ If I were a doctor

☐ Thank you letters to our guest speakers

WORK PROGRAM: Extract 2

Topic: Health

Function	Suggested Structures — Personal Cleanliness			
Describing Bathtime Describing Hair Care Indentifying Clean and Dirty Giving reasons for Hanky use Expressing approval/ disapproval	1. Bathtime Frequency adverbs — often (spash)	2. Hair care Frequency adverbs — always — Simple present — brush/comb/wash	3. Clean hands Fingernails — these/those	4. Use of handkerchief Frequency adverbs — always, never
Describing suitable clothing Expressing desires and needs Expressing satisfaction/ dissatisfaction Expressing obligation	5. Suitable clothing Time clauses: when it's hot, when it's cold	6. Importance of sleep Need/Want	7. Neat and Tidy appearance Like/don't like Simple present	8. Cleanliness of environment Frequency adverb always/never must and always, never
Expressing social attitudes Talking about specific occupations Explaining processes	9. Good manners Always please — Thank you — May I — I'm sorry — I beg your pardon — Excuse me	10. Care of teeth Time phrases — in the morning/ before bed — Frequency adverbs. Irregular nouns — eg. tooth/teeth 1st Conditional Comparatives	11. The dentist Present simple — 1st Conditional — if we have a toothache we see the dentist Temporal conjunctions — When I go — (Simple present)	12. The Doctor As for Dentist

93

You can see that the two programs approach the planning of the same topic in quite different ways. In the first extract, the teacher has started by listing fairly typical activities associated with the theme of cleanliness and hygiene. The list reflects the teacher's concern to provide very rich and varied input for the children and to incorporate into her planning a range of opportunities for the children to use language for real purposes in authentic communication, for example, to visit the doctor or to thank the guest speakers. The activities are grouped and ordered more or less according to the concepts involved, but there appears to have been no attempt to make these concepts explicit nor to identify the specific language forms that would be needed to carry out the tasks. In a sense, the teacher has planned what the children in her class will *do* but not what they will need to *say* or *write* — the focus of the planning is on using language to do things. It seems to be assumed that the children will 'pick-up' the language simply by using it.

The second extract is very different. The teacher appears to have started her planning with a breakdown of the topics that the children will need to be exposed to and her planning of content tends to be much more specific than in the first extract. Some of the topics also tend to look too 'basic' for the Anglo-Australian classroom, for example, a whole topic on good manners or the use of the handkerchief! It is only when you remember that the majority of children in this school are from a very different background that such topic choices appear to make much more sense, as the content of both these topics is very culture-bound. The scope of the topics is also, in many ways, more limited and a lot more time seems to have been allocated to activities.

An even more distinctive feature of this teacher's notes, however, is the emphasis on the language that will be introduced with each topic. The language has been analysed according to its grammatical structure, its function and the specific vocabulary involved. Certain patterns of language are highlighted and repeated, for example, adverbs of frequency and simple present tense. It is clear that the focus of this planning is on language *development,* although still in a highly contextualized way.

Put the two approaches together — and you have a very balanced and rich program for *all* students.

Many schools have expended a great deal of time, energy and thought developing policies that reflect this new classroom reality. Compare the following extracts from the language policies of the previously mentioned schools.

LANGUAGE POLICY: Extract 1

Children will learn language when

— they are immersed in and surrounded by language and experiences which are supported by language

— they have language demonstrated to them regularly and are guided towards new ways of communicating through a variety of media

— they are responsible for the appropriateness of their own language

— they are given ample opportunity to employ daily the whole range of language skills

— they are actively engaged in the teaching situation and this engagement is constantly monitored by staff

---

LANGUAGE POLICY: Extract 2

Children must achieve a standard of communicative competence that will enable them to

— participate and learn within a mainstream classroom

— select appropriate language and mannerisms when communicating and interacting with peers, teachers and other members of the school community

— function adequately within the wider community sphere

— The school must recognise the special cultural and cognitive needs of those students with interrupted or no previous schooling

---

It is clear that, while both policies emphasise that children need to be able to communicate effectively, only the second extract actually talks of *developing* communicative competence.

Again, the focus in the first document appears to be on providing opportunities for language use — it seems to be assumed that language development will then follow naturally. The children are 'responsible for the appropriateness of their own language' and although there is the suggestion that they will be 'guided', there is little sense of active intervention on the part of the teacher in the language learning process. Rather, the document simply lists conditions for language learning.

In contrast, the second extract evokes a much more conscious and active language *learner* who is operating in a range of very clearly defined socially constructed contexts. This extract, in fact, has a very powerful social justice orientation that is totally lacking from the first policy document.

These examples highlight crucial differences in emphasis between the two schools. Both at the classroom level and at the whole school level, in policy and in practice, quite different, although easily reconcilable, views of the language learner and the language learning task emerge. The first school focuses on suggesting means to a vaguely-defined end, the second focuses on the ends themselves and the language syllabus that is required to meet these ends.

The rhetoric of the 'whole language' and 'natural learning' approaches tends to suggest that children are doing a lot of language work, but, in many ways, the reality is quite different. Language and learning are taken to be synonymous, that is, if the child is placed in a rich learning environment, he will acquire language. This might be the case for many Anglo-Australian children from literate, middle-class backgrounds but it is clearly mistaken when applied to ESL children. Models such as Cambourne's conditions for language learning fail to take into account the specialised needs of ESL children, thus multiethnic schools find it very difficult to develop their students' 'natural' potential.

A whole language primary classroom that incorporates the principles of natural learning can be modified relatively simply to meet the needs of all children but only if schools take a long, hard look at their policies and practices.

The negotiation of the joint mainstream/ESL program becomes a key role of the ESL teacher. At both the whole school level and at the classroom level, the ESL teacher must be involved in and inform the planning, implementation and evaluation of the curriculum (Ministry of

Education, Victoria 1988). As well, she must help to establish supportive administrative structures and policies and a positive, collaborative teaching and learning environment (Davison 1992)

The battle continues to convince the educational community and policy-makers in Australia that TESOL can be both a method and an area of learning , both 'English' and yet a language other than English, both similar to and yet different from good generalist primary teaching. In some schools and systems there have been ground-breaking achievements, in too many other settings ESL learners appear caught in a time warp.

Snapshots — From now 'til ....?

A primary classroom in a Catholic school

Three teachers are planning a unit of work for the infant grade while the Principal takes the class. One teacher is a qualified ESL specialist, another is the Community Language teacher, the third is a generalist classroom teacher. They are planning a unit on *Food*. Some of the topics seem very simple, for example, a whole session on foods that we eat, another on table manners, but this is a school with many Indo-Chinese students and the school-wide sociolinguistic profile has shown up this topic as universal yet with different interpretations for *all* students. The simple, concrete exploration of cultural values and the way in which they are constructed is explored and questioned, for example, through looking at the importance attached to dairy products in different societies and the reasons for cross-cultural differences. A lot of time is allocated to predicting and recycling activities and the language used in each lesson is analysed according to its linguistic structure, its function and the specific vocabulary involved. These are compared with the goals for such learners at this key stage on the National ESL Profile. Certain patterns of language are highlighted and repeated, for example instructions, adverbs of frequency and simple present tense. It is clear that the focus of this planning is on systematic language *development*, not just opportunities for use.

A Science lesson at a State primary school

Two teachers are standing in front of a class of eleven year olds from a variety of different language backgrounds. One seems to be the mainstream teacher — she is taking the whole class for a brainstorming activity grouping and classifying words to do with the topic on **Force**. A young girl gives an answer in Vietnamese and the cross-age tutor interprets for the teacher. Just then, another teacher steps forward and hands out some worksheets, asking the students to form groups to decide what equipment they might need for the experiment. The first teacher, the ESL teacher, moves to a group at the front and helps an Iraqi boy explain some instructions to his Australian-born friend.

A classroom in a P-12 college.

A group of four ESL students is standing in front of a Grade Five class. They are much older than the other children, who wait expectantly. The ESL students talk briefly to each other in Khmer. They have only been at the language centre in the school for a few months but will probably stay until the end of the year as they have missed out on so much schooling in the Thai refugee camp. They are going to describe Ankor Wat to the class and have some lovely hand-made posters to show to the children. They have rehearsed what they will say many times with the ESL and Art teachers while working on a topic on **Description** but they still feel nervous. They hope that the excited children will not ask them too many questions!

Challenges for the future

The development of coherent and effective ESL programs in Australian schools has been a long and on-going struggle, but a struggle which has had some of its ferocity softened by this country's relative prosperity and tolerance, its long history of migration and the contribution of its ethnic communities to public life, not to mention its decade of Labour government. It remains to be seen whether Australian schools can continue to develop as one effective model of the integration of ESL into the mainstream.

References

Campbell, W.J. & McMeniman, M. (1985) *Bridging the Language Gap: Ideals and Realities Pertaining to Learning English as a Second Language (ESL)*, Canberra: Commonwealth Schools Commission.

Cleland, B. & Evans, R. (1986) *Learning English Through General Science: Teacher's Book*, Melbourne: Longman.

Cambourne, B. (1988) *The Whole Story: Natural Learning and the Acquisition of Literacy*, Ashton Scholastic, Auckland.

Davison, C. (1992) 'Look Out: Eight Fatal Flaws in Team and Support Teaching', *TESOL in Context*, Vol. 2, No. 1, Australian Council of TESOL Associations.

Davison, C. (1990) ' When nature needs some help! The natural learning approach and the teaching of ESL in the primary school' *TESOL in Context*, Vol. 1, No. 1, Australian Council of TESOL Associations.

Gibbons, P. (1991) *Learning to Learn in a Second Language*, Sydney: Primary English Teaching Association.

Kay, A. (1990) 'Teacher Development and ESL in the Mainstream', *TESOL in Context*, Vol. 1, No. 1, Australian Council of TESOL Associations.

Lo Bianco, J (1987) *The National Policy on Languages*, Canberra: Australian Government Printing Service.

Martin, J (1978) *The Migrant Presence*, Sydney: Allen & Unwin.

Ministry of Education (1988) *Teaching English as a Second Language: A Support Document for the English Language Framework*, Melbourne, Australia.

Chapter 7

Pragmatic biculturalism and the primary school teacher

Ann Knight

Governments world-wide are redefining educational opportunity to fit even more closely the ideology and requirements of the market economy. To achieve this in Britain the content of the curriculum is now decided by central government, which has also taken a tighter control of funding and resources. Thus the National Curriculum and management restructuring now in place dictate to a large degree the classroom teacher's input. But despite the government slogan of 'education for all' the quality of education has become increasingly variable. The effect of an education policy which rewards the achiever and the achieving school also results in restricting educational opportunity for those children whose lives have already been directly and adversely affected by other government policies. They have unemployed parents, inadequate housing, a poor environment, a contracting health service and restricted leisure facilities. They are now progressively penalised for the lower attainment levels that are in fact the result of government policies. Committed teachers in inner-city schools wishing to develop the abilities of their pupils, so that performance can match potential, must consider all strategies to achieve this. This chapter suggests that one of these strategies should be a rigorous analysis and development of bicultural acquisition to enable pupils to function with greater skill and understanding within the mainstream culture which controls their lives.

Biculturalism

It is important for teachers in inner-city schools to recognise that their pupils are not only living in a multicultural society, they are also living amid a mainstream culture which is different from that of their home culture. It is this mainstream culture that controls their lives. It is clear that in a society so structured, many children need to be supported in their development of bicultural skills and understanding in order to succeed.

Culture is, of course, more than food and festivals:

it comprises all aspects of human behaviour that are not innate reflexes or instincts. It is everything men derive from nature or the human environment. It includes language and logic, religion and philosophy, morality and law as well as the manufacture and use of tools, clothes, houses and even the selection of food to eat. All this men must learn from their fellows in society. (Childe, 1952)

Certainly when we consider the culture of a society remote in time and space, Aztecs in the past, Tangkhul Nagas today, these are the aspects of its culture we would attempt to define, recognising that a dynamic interaction between the different cultural aspects of that society and other cultures and the surrounding environment had brought the society its distinct culture. Since cultures are dynamic processes, they continue to evolve.

Self-sufficient rural communities possess a relatively unified culture at any time: traditions, beliefs, social systems, economic activity etc. all exist and take place on or around the home base. In many rural Asian communities, for example, law is experienced on-site. An inter- or intra-village dispute is usually solved at that level, without the intervention of state judicial procedures. Alternative off-site culture, although it exists, is not a frequent experience. Therefore the ideology and social organisation of public site culture, with accompanying social interaction codes (appropriate behaviour patterns expressed in language, content of interaction, courtesies, body language etc.), do not need to be developed. This is not to deny an ability to handle different interaction codes effectively. On the contrary, in many rural cultures social interaction codes are particularly elaborate and defined. They exist to structure all encounters and interactions with behaviour and language appropriate for the relationship between those involved. Thus a Bangladeshi woman must use different and predefined interactional codes with her husband's elder brother from those she uses with his younger brother; different again between his mother and father; different again with neighbours of varying age, sex and status. These codes determine not only the form and style of the interaction but also its content.

In most urban societies a more fragmented culture exists. Life is experienced at different levels, with a broad division into home and public culture. Home culture encompasses religion, belief, customs, traditions, language, private morality, dress, diet and appropriate social organisation patterns. Public culture contains state and economic organisation patterns, with their appropriate interactional codes. It has its own social and language codes which derive from those of home culture but develop with their own feedback dynamic. The degree of divergence between home and public cultures varies for the different social classes in that society. Public culture approximates more closely to the home culture of the middle classes, whose members are of course more likely to be both in control of and empowered by that culture. They organise and in greater proportion benefit from public culture.

For families moving from rural to urban environments — the experience of many immigrant families to Britain up to the end of the 1970s — the dislocation affects their traditionally unified culture by redefining and limiting its functioning. This must be recognised so that the impact of Western culture on such families can be better understood. Home culture is retained and often becomes a focus of power in the search for self-identity and self-esteem. But mainstream public culture has to be accepted to a great degree, with its accompanying acculturation, since the incoming groups have no alternative public culture.

When we consider the implications of this for working-class children and those with minority languages it is clear that they need to feel confident within public culture as well as to understand alternative home cultures. For this to happen they must learn how public culture functions, not only at a structural but also at an ideological level. If pupils were studying an external culture such an analysis would be a basic requirement. How much more important when they are considering the culture that controls their own lives.

Biculturalism and the primary school teacher

Ideally, children of all classes should develop bicultural skills and understanding. It is a matter of urgency for working-class children, and especially for black Afro-Caribbean and Asian children. Home culture variation will usually be greater for black Afro-Caribbean and Asian families while public culture can be a relatively new experience for some families, and something to which incoming parents or grandparents had to adjust. They were likely to have had no role except that of controllee in what was a white man's world. For the black or Asian child, too, there are the added dimensions to public culture of institutional racism inherent in the system; while between home and public cultures they experience the racist attacks which are nurtured by the inequality derived from public culture. These aspects of children's experience must be progressively examined by children and teachers in the process of bicultural acquisition. Although this is a pragmatic response, it need not necessarily imply collusion with mainstream culture, as it is possible to combine the development of biculturalism with an ability to analyse the structure of the culture which requires its use.

The acquisition of bicultural skills

While many inner-city primary schools respond to the theory and practice of bilingual development, similar strategies are seldom in place for bicultural acquisition. Few schools control or structure bicultural development, or even recognise a need to do so. In most inner-city schools an immersion process takes place, but as this is not the result of a policy decision, the effects and implications of the process are not analysed. Within such schools, conservatist-liberal interpretations of public culture are in place. Benign curriculum projects about 'people who help us', including the role of the doctor, dentist, nurse, police and shopkeeper present mainstream assessments of their roles, and frequently bear little resemblance to the pupils' own encounters with such figures.

Traditionally primary schools do not analyse with pupils the reality of public culture as experienced by young children, nor do they attempt to develop bicultural or analytical skills which help children to understand why these structures are in place. Aspects of public culture such as long school waiting lists or high unemployment may affect a school directly (unemployment=free school meal qualification=extra funding), but the impact on pupils of having cousins at home with no school to attend, or having unemployed fathers, uncles or brothers, is unlikely to be raised in the classroom.

In the same way few primary schools analyse or develop their pupils' awareness of alternative forms of white home culture, though multicultural education may offer positive reinforcement of other, more remote cultures. For the black Afro-Caribbean or Asian child the process of decoding different forms of white home culture can be particularly confusing. Children are surrounded by different levels and forms of white home culture. The books they read, the stories they hear, the TV soaps and sitcoms they watch, all present a range of home cultures which often seem to bear little relation to their own experience of random street encounters.

Strategies for teaching bicultural skills and understanding

How then can primary school teachers support pupils' acquisition of an effective biculturalism? We should first recognise that teachers need to understand the process of cultural and bicultural acquisition, and to define mainstream British culture. Teachers and schools should analyse their own culture and its likely impact on their professional responsibilities. Most British teachers are white and monolingual, and come to the inner-city school with professional skills and specific experiences. Most are monoculturate, although if they come from a working-class background they will have had to develop a range of bicultural skills and therefore will be more likely to relate to the position of their pupils. This will be most markedly the case for black Afro-Caribbean or Asian teachers. Most teachers will recognise that they are working with children who possess home cultures different from their own. They will need to appreciate that working-class children will already have had frequent encounters with mainstream culture, but only in an unempowered role. Such experiences are unlikely to have been analysed systematically with them. For black Afro-Caribbean and Asian children the racism frequently implicit in

105

public encounters is unlikely to have been discussed explicitly. These encounters will probably have resulted in their forming a very different perception of public culture from that of the teacher. The children, then, will already have become involved in bicultural acquisition, though in an unstructured, non-analytical manner.

The children in our schools are members of particular cultures living in a specific cultural environment while engaging in interactive relationships with those of the same and other cultures. To comprehend this, teachers should be prepared to learn about their pupils' home culture through a range of local research strategies. Too often the home visit is now seen as an activity specific only to the home-school liaison teacher, pastoral care teacher, link worker or community worker. Classroom teachers may feel discouraged from making their own contacts with the community; but to meet families on their home ground can only be beneficial for teachers, parents and pupils. Insights can be gained into the children's home culture, and discussions in the home can often reveal the interface between home and public culture. Such local visiting reflects local particular experience rather than giving more generalised non-personal information. Teachers will also need to build up detailed knowledge of the school's local area in an ongoing profile. In this way teachers can begin to work out the implications of the facts of public culture (unemployment rates, housing, leisure facilities etc.) on the lives of their pupils. To gain clear insights into the local area teachers can often discuss specific questions with community and advice workers in the voluntary and statutory sectors, as well as with community leaders. In this way they can begin to develop an overview of how public culture impacts on the area as a whole, while also providing insights into home culture. The effects of their relationship between home and public culture on individual pupils will be learned through discussion and interaction in the classroom.

When primary school teachers decide that the development of biculturalism should form an integral part of the classroom environment, they realise that this fits easily with a commitment to interactive education. As with multicultural education, it can provide a lens through which to view experience and information, and the interactive format stimulates the discussion about what has been revealed. Interactive education provides the structure for a development of learning which stimulates pupils to move forward:

> In classrooms organised for interactive pedagogy teacher-pupil talk changes role relationship... there is the potential for teachers to see themselves as part of one single educational complex of teachers and students all having better access to each others' ideas, thoughts, purposes and intentions. (Levine, 1990)

Interactive education offers teachers a means of constructing a rigorous and supportive pedagogy which can follow natural learning patterns and is supportive for pupils' learning. This interactive process is vital. If bicultural support were offered in a didactic teaching framework the process would almost certainly fail as it would lack the element of trust that is necessary for mutual discussion of home and street experiences. We can consider two sets of teacher-responses to children's 'news' contributions:

Example 1: A child says 'my father gets his money from the post office.'

Teacher-response (a) 'Your father is unemployed so the government gives him money to help him.'

Teacher-response (b) The teacher initiates discussion about the reasons why there is no longer enough work in the area, and where benefit money comes from.

Example 2: A child says 'My sister is crying because her husband didn't get entry.'

Teacher-response (a) 'That is because the immigration laws don't let everyone come into this country.'

Teacher-response (b) The teacher initiates discussion around shared experience — are immigration laws fair?

Is it fair that if the child's sister has a baby her husband can more easily gain entry?

Example 3: A child says 'We had burglars and we rang the police but they didn't come.'

Teacher-response (a) 'The police try their best to help us but they are very busy.'

Teacher-response (b) The teacher initiates a discussion around shared experiences of the police and possible reasons for their behaviour.

Example 4: A child says 'We have got new neighbours and we don't like them because they are Pakis.'

Teacher-response (a) 'That's not very friendly, there are nice people in all countries and you really shouldn't call people Pakis.'

Teacher-response (b) The teacher initiates discussion about attitudes to name-calling and cultural identity.

It is clear that establishing an interactive format to discuss these events, which almost all involve encounters with public culture, can help the teacher and the children to move forward in their bicultural development. In each case response (a) adopts the didactic approach of a conservatist-liberal teacher, and may simply leave the children feeling alienated so that personal experiences would hardly be brought to the teacher again; it is only in an atmosphere of mutual trust and respect that private experiences will be brought out for public scrutiny.

As children mature and become more adept at cultural code-switching such interactive strategies can be used in drama, role-play and creative writing to support biculturalism either by reproducing actual experiences or by presenting those felt to be appropriate for specific cultural contexts. Recognition of the structure of another culture develops analytical skills which support pupils in curriculum subjects such as history and geography, as pupils become skilled at looking for the 'reasons why' rather than the 'facts that' a given situation or state occurs.

It may be suggested that much of what has been described here is better carried out by multicultural and/or anti-racist strategies. Multicultural education has much to commend it in terms of enabling teacher and children to look at the world beyond the classroom, reinforcing children's understanding of a range of cultures and developing respect for and awareness of different backgrounds. It is a strategy which can validate minority group children's home culture, and is an important component in developing self-belief. It can therefore be a valuable and successful strategy, though it is not always rigorously structured in its presentation. However, multicultural education can too often simply involve aspects of home cultures which are easily identifiable and are considered in discrete areas such as religion, festivals, food, homes, dress. It can thus marginalise other important aspects of culture as well as failing to prepare pupils for the full impact of mainstream culture. It is, in fact, a strategy endorsed by conservatist-liberal ideology, as it seldom challenges complacency.

Advocates of an anti-racist approach may argue that in seeking to develop bicultural dexterity a bicultural approach seems to involve collusion with a system which is irretrievably flawed, and should be replaced. However much we may wish for such a change in society, children cannot afford to wait until a new system is in place. The bicultural skills and understanding suggested here would develop together with an analytical ability to recognise the inherent inequality of the present system. These skills seem to be appropriate for all working-class children, and especially for black Afro-Caribbean and Asian children in Britain; surely any strategy which could enable children to make further use of their limited and limiting educational opportunity has to be considered.

Alienation

The reinforcement of home culture from the early years can establish children's self-belief, while the development of biculturalism gradually prepares pupils to function with confidence in public culture. The analytical skills that can be developed through a guided interactive process which measures mainstream culture against the cultural experience of young children benefits all aspects of learning. If this process is absent pupils can become alienated as they perceive their irrelevance to the culture of the school. Anderton (1993) found that teachers in a Birmingham school had little knowledge of their pupils' cultural background, frequently finding that teachers 'don't ever identify them as anything other than children'; in interviewing pupils she found that they were keenly aware of their teachers' ignorance:

> Student A: I'm a Bengali, I'm proud of that. I'm Bengali but I'm not when in school, it doesn't matter, they don't care what you are.

For many young people street culture offers a more appealing alternative to the public culture that surrounds them. The apparent control and empowerment it offers young people who have been marginalised and managed by public culture has to be attractive. Unable to assess its market economy manipulations, they recognise only the opportunity for a withdrawal into a peer group culture that synthesises home cultures while allowing particular local emphases. Most young people are confident about their cultural identity, so that the 'between two cultures' confusion of the 1970s and early 1980s is unlikely to be a factor in their search for self-worth. Home culture in fact may form the basis of the street culture which they enter. This is positive in so far as it offers a viable alternative to the culture they are rejecting. But since it has no dimension of public culture empowerment it is difficult to sustain a life-style on these terms without it becoming static or even negative. Opting out of a mainstream culture which they do not understand, and by which they are both marginalised and manipulated can happen at a time when young people are educationally most vulnerable. It will then simply reinforce the pattern of disadvantage. No doubt at a time of high unemployment and recession the self-destructing underclass can be viewed with equanimity by those whose policies have brought it into being, but as educators we must share some responsibility for ourselves being manipulated into allowing it to happen.

Summary

In order to provide equal educational opportunity for all pupils, teachers need to recognise that schools form part of a public culture which is skewed in favour of the white middle-class. For children whose home culture is very different from that of their school the demands of playing according to the rules are great. They surely have the right to be taught these rules, and the skills required for success, even if they eventually decide that it is not a game they wish to play. Education is for many the only route out of injustice, and if bicultural strategies can provide maps of the territory to be encountered on the road to fulfilment they should be encouraged. By demystifying the landscape, by developing the traveller's skill at reading coded signs, bicultural education can support pupils' progress. Too many of those in power see such strategies as a challenge to their authority. But for many teachers who recognise the gross waste of potential that occurs at present such strategies must be worth attempting. In the 1980s the Bangladesh Rural Advancement Committee showed a group of visiting Birmingham teachers a village project set up as a joint initiative by the villagers and themselves. BRAC told us that 'We lived here in the village for a long time before they would work with us. Why should they trust us? Our lives are so different.' If pupils and their parents are not quite so wary in inner-city Britain, at least they continually assess teachers' motivation to become part of their new environment. Teachers who recognise this will abandon their own preconceptions of superiority as they realise the opportunity for their own bicultural development alongside that of their pupils.

References

Anderton, E. (1993) *Bangladeshi Pupils' Experience of Secondary Schooling* Unpublished M.Ed. thesis, University of East Anglia.

Childe, G. (1952) *Social Education* (Watts & Co.)

Levine, J. (1990) *Bilingual Learners and the Mainstream Curriculum* Falmer, Lewes

Chapter 8

Bilingualism, biculturalism and learning in early years classrooms

Stephen Nyakatawa and Iram Siraj-Blatchford

The National Curriculum and Bilingual Learners

DES Circular 5/89 hailed the UK National Curriculum as an 'entitlement curriculum'. According to the Education Reform Act (1988) all pupils in maintained schools are entitled to a curriculum that is 'balanced and broadly-based' and which:

● promotes the spiritual, moral, cultural, mental and physical development of pupils at the school and of society and

● prepares such pupils for the opportunities, responsibilities and experiences of adult life (DES 1989: para. 16).

The circular (1989) continues in the same broad terms ...

> 'It is intended that the curriculum should reflect the culturally diverse society to which pupils belong and of which they will become adult members(DES 1989: para. 17)

Although this was seen as a positive step forward, the circular was lacking in practical strategies for teachers to use in their classrooms.

> The official agenda is that all children should acquire the same skills and knowledge through their participation in the classroom tasks (Alton-Lee and Nuthall, 1993:59).

In this context it is important to recognise that bilingual pupils have knowledge they cannot yet articulate in English. The teacher's task is to tap into the pupils' existing knowledge and use it as a basis for their teaching strategies. Using bilingual pupils' home language and cultural context in the teaching/learning environment is an essential initial strategy. The National Curriculum was not so specific and it had been suggested that many bilingual pupils may be left out of the National Curriculum Standard Assessment Tasks (SATs) because of 'inadequate' English, although there is emerging evidence that this has rarely been applied at Key Stage One.

Language makes accessible culture, culture includes the bilingual pupil's experience, and experience shapes knowledge. These interconnections were not made explicit for bilingual/bicultural learners.

The crucial question to ask here is how teachers take into account bilingual pupils' linguistic and cultural differences and what guidance, if any, they have had from the former National Curriculum Council. Culture, identity, knowledge, experience and language are so closely interwoven that it does not seem possible to enhance and key into bilingual pupils' culture and identity through English alone, particularly in the early years of primary education. As Dodson (1988) argues,

> If the child's preferred language is kept out of the classroom, the child will resort to private bilingual inner speech, because he must, but he will do so guiltily and consequently insufficiently and imperfectly. This will affect the pupil's ability to engage in profitable teacher-pupil, pupil-pupil interactions so crucial for his proper concept development (1988:16)

If teaching strategies encourage, value and support the use of bilingual pupils' home language, the children are more likely to share their language and culture freely without feeling that they are the centre of attention. The home language then becomes the tool by which the initial negotiation of meanings is carried out, and the learning environment is transformed for the children. An experienced bilingual teacher may also be crucial in enabling timid bilingual pupils to open up their linguistic and cultural world because the bilingual teacher can enter the pupil's culture through language. The negotiation of meaning is facilitated because there already exists a body of shared cultural experiences and knowledge. As Wood has argued,

> children's knowledge is often a product of the joint construction of understanding by the child and more expert members of his culture (1988:16)

For these joint activities to materialise, it is assumed that a knowledge base is shared between the adult and the child. Language helps understanding. It also transmits the cultural values during the adult-child interactions with the adult sanctioning culturally accepted behaviour, norms and values. In all societies infants interact with parents or adults in an effort to come to a shared understanding of the meanings conveyed through language as well as learning the rules of language. An examination of how infants and adults interact will help illuminate how language and knowledge are acquired.

Language Learning and culture

Vygotsky (1986) maintained that children's experience of language is socially orientated from the outset and that the social environment plays a significant role in the acquisition of language and other dimensions of cognitive development. Language, culture and environment are interdependent. How, then, does the social environment influence the child's acquisition of language?

Language acquisition begins before children utter their first recognisable word. According to Bruner (1985) language acquisition begins when the mother and infant form and define an interaction that can serve as a microcosm for communicating in a shared reality. The exchanges that occur within this framework help children learn the 'rules' of grammar, learn how to refer and convey meaning. The role of the mother is to structure the input and fine-tune the child's language development. This process also involves negotiating a shared and familiar context.

Bruner (1985) called the input provided by the mother or other adults to the infant the Language Acquisition Support System (LASS). This is external to the child and is influenced by the social environment.

This makes it possible for the infant to enter the linguistic community — and at the same time the culture to which the language gives access (Bruner 1985:19).

Culture is constituted of symbolic procedures, concepts and distinctions that can only be made in language. It is constituted for the child in the very act of mastering language. *Language, in consequence, cannot be understood save in its cultural setting* (Bruner 1985:134, our emphasis).

During the child's early years at school, teachers/adults may continue to enhance the LASS in ways that tend to complement the language and culture of the home and that of the school. There may be no significant differences between the language and culture of the home and that of the school:

So members of the same culture will define situations in similar ways and endow them with agreed meanings (Nias et al 1989:12).

However, due to cultural and linguistic differences between the home and school, some pupils may experience difficulties in the classroom. For example, for a bilingual child whose first language is Panjabi, participation in classroom activities through a white, English teacher can cause communication as well as cross-cultural problems. Studies (Ingham, 1982; Oglivy et al, 1990; Wright, 1992; Biggs and Edwards, 1992) confirm that adult-child interactions with bilingual pupils of South Asian or African-Caribbean descent were very low compared to their white peers. Two possible reasons are advanced, language differences and teachers' racist attitudes towards pupils from South Asian and African-Caribbean backgrounds.

To elaborate on this, Alton-Lee and Nuthall (1993) emphasise that teachers and pupils have their own cultural perspectives shaped by their gender, class and race and these are not necessarily shared or made public. The significance of these differences is ignored by teachers when they declare that they treat all their pupils equally (Biggs and Edwards, 1992). Bilingual pupils' language and culture is not acknowledged.

Children's individual personalities are, of course, also an important influence on how they communicate in class. But it is meaningless to talk of anyone's individual personality existing independently of their experience of being a boy, a black person, Welsh or whatever (Mercer, 1985:30)

Therefore, bilingual pupils' language and culture need to be acknowledged if individual learning needs are to be met. The main issue being explored in this chapter is whether bilingual pupils can access the National Curriculum more effectively through monolingual, monocultural teachers or through bilingual teachers.

There is also a need to question further what bilingual pupils learn about their own identity, values, self-worth and learning potential, in contexts where teachers may hold racist attitudes and assumptions (however unintentional).

Classroom Interactions and Learning

It seems likely that where there is a close linguistic and cultural match between bilingual pupils and their teachers, classroom interactions and communication will be less problematic. For bilingual pupils, encountering classroom activities through a suitably experienced bilingual teacher may enhance overall learning progress. Classroom discourse is unlikely to be hindered by communication or cross-cultural misunderstandings. An analogy could be drawn here between white working-class pupils and their attempts to decode the middle-class language and culture of the classroom.

At this point, Bernstein's (1970:120) often quoted statement is worth repeating:

If the culture of the teacher is to become part of the consciousness of the child, then the culture of the child must first be in the consciousness of the teacher (1970:120).

This may mean that the teacher must be able to understand the child's dialect rather than deliberately attempting to change it. Many of the contexts of our schools are unwittingly drawn from aspects of the symbolic world of the middle-class and so when children step into school they are stepping into a symbolic system which does not provide for them a link with their life outside.

117

Sleeter and Grant (1988) have argued that more attention should be paid to the social backgrounds of teachers. They are convinced that teachers' own social origins, mainly white and middle class, limit their conceptions and understanding of race, class and gender inequalities. They further commented, as have others (Siraj-Blatchford 1993), that there were very few teachers from the ethnic minorities. What has emerged so far from the preceding argument, is that a difference in social backgrounds between teachers and pupils could have a negative effect on pupils' classroom interactions and learning progress. The lack of ethnic minority teachers in the teaching force means that bilingual pupils have very few teachers of their own ethnic background to regard as role models.

Also, for bilingual pupils the main differences between them and their white teachers are not just limited to class, language and culture but also to race. As was indicated earlier, race is a determining factor in the quality and quantity of child-adult interactions in early years at school (Ingham, 1982; Oglivy et al, 1990; Wright, 1992; Biggs and Edwards, 1992). This chapter considers the effect of mismatches in perceptions, expectations and attitudes between teachers and bilingual pupils in the early stages of the primary school.

Before children enter school they will have acquired pre-school assumptions and attitudes within a specific cultural, social and linguistic framework. The transition from home to school will be smoother if these experiences are compatible with the school's and the teachers'. It has been shown that this is not always the case (Bernstein, 1970; Grant and Sleeter, 1985) due to social class, race, gender, linguistic and cultural differences between teachers and pupils.

In short,

> the exchange of meaning through speech is dependent on the sharing of an inter-subjective field in which the intentions and perceptions of each partner together with *a world of shared meanings* must be represented both in the speaker and hearer for any exchange of meaning to be successful (Shields, 1978:537).

During the 1960s the research focus shifted from the materials used by the teacher and their teaching methods to teacher talk with a whole class. Studies by Bellack, 1966; Flanders, 1970; Sinclair and Coulthard, 1974, focused on the observation and analysis of the teachers' linguistic strategies and the resulting meanings as interpreted by the class.

However, teachers have the ability to exert considerable control over classroom communication in terms of what is said, by whom, to whom and how it is said. Gorden Wells (1986) summarised the nature of most teacher-pupil interactions, arguing that they follow a regular pattern called Exchange which can be divided into three main parts as follows; an *Initiation* (by the teacher), a *Response* (by the child) and a further evaluation of what the child has said or *Feedback* (from the teacher), IRF for short. IRF can dominate classroom talk, leaving pupils with very few opportunities to ask questions or initiate interactions. It is particularly pertinent for bilingual pupils to initiate interactions because they can tease out the language and culture of the classroom to find out what is appropriate. The monolingual teacher can use bilingual pupils as a resource. Therefore these pupils should be allowed, during classroom discourse, to demonstrate the knowledge and skills they bring with them to the learning environment. Learning should be seen as a collaborative partnership between the teacher and the pupil where the lines of communication are open.

Neil Mercer (1985) analysed the likely consequences in the classroom if teachers and pupils do not 'know' each other well culturally:

> ... some children come to school with a culturally specific style of communicative behaviour which is so different from that of their teachers, and of the education system in general, they they will not only make different interpretations of specific aspects of communication like tone of voice, purpose of questions, non-verbal signals and so on; they will also sometimes behave in such ways that a *teacher who is not of their culture is liable to misunderstand them* (1985:29, our emphasis).

Pupil-Pupil Interactions and Collaborative Group Work

Mercer's (1985) analysis above shows that effective communication in the classroom is essential for learning and social interactions. In the past, young pupils have tended to be seen as egocentric and classroom communications have therefore tended to be individualistic in nature. Further exploration and criticism of Piaget's theories by Margaret Donaldson (1978) and others has shown that the cognitive and social development of the young child are intertwined, and therefore greater emphasis should be placed on communication between individuals, especially in the process of problem solving. The use of collaborative groups for learning should be encouraged.

Mercer (1985) identified that children working together in small groups were able to:

● talk more freely

● take greater risks in their thinking

● take greater initiative in posing questions

● relate their own experiences to the new learning

● make use of home languages other than English

● provide linguistic support for each other including the child learning English as a second language (Bruner's LASS)

● carry the support and help they often give each other in their social relationships into their schooling.

The ORACLE study (1980) found that although most children in their sample were organised in groups in the classroom, they worked individually — only 10 of all activities scrutinised called for communication and collaboration between pupils. The researchers concluded that group work was under-used.

Galton and Williamson (1992) in their more recent study on group work, extracted the following key points from their review of the literature. When children sit in groups they tend to achieve more if working towards a common objective. Co-operative group work seems to improve pupils' self-esteem and motivation.

For bilingual pupils, particularly, participation in whole-class lessons initially involves public risk-taking and managing the consequences of failing or succeeding. The risk of failure can be reduced within the confines and security of collaborative group work. Through peer-tutoring and support, the bilingual child learns the language and culture of the classroom and how to communicate cross-culturally. Vygotsky (1934) believed that children learn best in social situations when they are interacting with others who can *support and nurture their efforts.*

Galton and Williamson (1992) identified factors which have a positive effect on pupil achievement. They suggested that groups should be of mixed ability and that such groups should be representative of the gender, racial and social class mix of the class. However, there have been some worrying recommendations from the various discussion documents (Alexander et al 1992, NCC 1993) which suggest that the new direction for the organisation and practice of class teachers is strongly towards more class teaching and subject specialism. The only kind of group work advocated is associated with ability setting.

Galton and Williamson (1992) found that children performed best in practical tasks as conversation was involved in these tasks. Problem-solving tasks had to have a clear, testable result. Open-ended tasks did not generate a high degree of collaboration; it appears that children accepted the first answer or they were unwilling to explore their ideas further or challenge each other's ideas. For successful group work, pupils must be taught how to collaborate effectively. Groups are not static. Groups that may work well in the short term will not necessarily produce similar results in the long term. Different group composition may be required for different tasks. Galton and Williamson also found that the nature of teacher feedback influenced group performance. Teacher feedback that was corrective, emphasising the correction of pupil errors tended to have a negative effect on group work because of the focus on failure. 'Critical' feedback which focused on the quality of pupils' work tended to encourage the pupils to work independently of teachers.

Although Galton and Williamson suggested that groups should represent the social class, gender and racial mix of the class, an exploration of how these factors might influence the performance of a group is not included. An investigation of ethnicity as a factor in collaborative group work would be a useful next stage in researching this issue. The use of collaborative group work can benefit bilingual pupils in the early years of education. Bilingual pupils may benefit because collaborative group work tends to enhance their confidence, self-esteem and oral language skills. The peer-tutoring and support provided within a small group removes to a large extent the fear of failing in public. Teachers could support bilingual pupils' efforts in collaborative group work by being sensitive in the feedback that they offer to pupils. A bilingual pupil is unlikely to complete a task if the teacher has to correct each error.

The former schools Examinations and Assessment Council (SEAC, 1993) encouraged teachers to use small groups in the assessment of bilingual pupils.

> Generally, children who share a language other than English or Welsh will benefit from working together. These children often switch to and from their their home language in the course of the activity. At the same time children who are not fluent in English or Welsh also benefit from being grouped with others of similar general ability. (SEAC, 1993 School Assessment Folder Key Stage One).

There is general agreement about the benefits of collaborative group work for all pupils; for bilingual pupils new to English, such a strategy is essential.

Teacher Perceptions, Attitudes and Expectations of Bilingual Children

According to Susan Foster (1990) children need to be in possession of three different types of knowledge in order to become effective communicators.

● *Personal knowledge* —i.e. knowledge about how other people see their (the childrens') world. If these perceptions are positive this will enhance their academic, social and emotional development. If the messages that bilinguals receive in the classroom about their language and culture are negative they will either attempt to reject their language and culture or they will perceive the learning environment to be irrelevant to their needs because it does not touch or build upon their everyday experience in a positive manner.

● *Social category knowledge* — i.e. knowledge about possible social relationships likely to exist between speaker and hearer which depend upon (a) the situation and (b) social categories such as sex, age, role, status and familiarity. We wish to add language and culture to these categories. It can therefore be deduced that a high degree of reciprocity of social category knowledge is desirable between the teacher and the pupil in order to maintain and sustain social interactions in the classroom environment. This is in some ways similar to the notion of shared meanings (Shields, 1978) that must exist between speaker and hearer, discussed earlier.

For bilingual pupils, the differences between their social category knowledge and their monolingual teachers may lead to less effective social interactions in the classroom (Mercer, 1985). For example, it is not culturally appropriate for bilingual pupils of South Asian origin to make eye contact or answer back when they are being reprimanded by an adult. Teachers have tended to label South Asian bilingual pupils wrongly, as quiet, shy, withdrawn or sly. Such an interpretation of bilingual pupils' behaviour not only serves to highlight the social category knowledge differences but also the teacher attitude to such differences. Bilingual pupils are expected to conform to the teacher's social category knowledge, hence cross-cultural misunderstandings can result. Rogoff and Mistry (1985) provide a further example of how a mismatch in conventions of social interactions can influence learning. They noted that it was culturally inappropriate for Mayan (American-Indian) children to speak freely to an adult. Hence, the difficulties that a Mayan child is likely to encounter in a western classroom environment become apparent.

● *Event knowledge* — i.e. knowledge about how events are *'normally'* organised, who says what to who and how they say it, for example *'familiar'* routines and conventions. A study cited earlier (Gordon Wells, 1986) noted that the IRF pattern of teacher-pupil communication left pupils with limited opportunities to engage in meaningful exchanges with the teacher or with other pupils.

For bilingual pupils, there are likely to be cross-cultural discrepancies in their event knowledge and their monolingual teacher's. What may appear normal and familiar in one cultural context may seem absurd in another.

For example, it is normal for Sikhs to take off their shoes before entering the'gurdwara' (temple) and for both males and females to have their heads covered. In most western cultures it is normal to greet each other by hugging, shaking hands or kissing. In South Asian culture physical contact between males and females when greeting each other is culturally inappropriate. What is normal is then culturally contextualised. In a multilingual, multicultural classroom environment, the learning process must involve negotiating and redefining what is perceived as normal or 'familiar' within that context and that of the wider society. In this process pupil-initiated interactions are crucial because bilingual pupils can guide their monolingual teachers and peers through aspects of the bilingual pupils' culture which they value.

This process of interaction requires the creation of a *common framework* for the co-ordination of action and exchange of information. Communication relies on the establishment of an intelligent context of interaction; this co-ordination facilitates generalisation, in that *new information has to be made compatible with the newcomer's existing knowledge* (Rogoff et al, (1984:322); quoted from Bornstein and Lamb (eds), *Developmental Psychology: An Advanced Textbook*).

It is therefore reasonable to claim that bilinguals need the security of their home language and cultural identity before they tackle the complexities of social interactions in the classroom. A bilingual teacher could facilitate the creation of a comfortable framework as suggested by Rogoff, in the pupil's home language. It could be difficult for a monolingual teacher to assess a bilingual pupil's current level of knowledge without reference to the bilingual pupil's home language.

The day-to-day classroom experiences of bilingual pupils need further investigation. Over twenty years ago, Rist (1970) conducted a longitudinal study of kindergarten children in an elementary school of a black neighbourhood in St Louis, USA, and evaluated their progress as they moved from the first grade to the second. Rist found that the white teachers in his sample employed roughly constructed categories which were perceived as prerequisites for pupils to succeed at school. He found that the teachers' initial and quick assessments were based on their first impressions of the pupils but these assessments hardly altered, in fact they became more formalised. It was noted that teacher-pupil classroom interactions were significantly influenced by the teacher assessments of their pupils. The differences between the groups of children were further reflected in both the seating arrangements and their performance. Thus by the second grade Rist noted:

'No matter how well a child in the lower reading groups might have read, she/he was destined to remain in the same reading group. This is, in a sense, another manifestation of the self-fulfilling prophecy in that a 'slow learner' has no option but to continue to be a slow learner, regardless of performance or potential (Rist, 1970:435).

A more recent project in the UK by Biggs and Edwards (1992) found that teachers interacted less frequently with ethnic minority children than with their white peers; they had fewer exchanges lasting more than thirty seconds with ethnic minority pupils. The teachers also spent less time with these pupils discussing the particular task which had been set. Like the pupils in Rist's sample, ethnic minority pupils were likely to underachieve in this context, regardless of performance or potential . However, both studies endorsed the strong influence that teacher perceptions, attitudes and expectations can have on teacher-pupil interactions and general learning progress. In a multilingual, multicultural learning environment, bilingual ethnic minority pupils form a ready-made category because of their minority status and their experience of racism.

It has already been pointed out how teachers can influence and control the quality and quantity of classroom interactions through Gordon Wells' IRF pattern. Given the teacher attitudes, perceptions and expectations just described, bilingual pupils could find themselves excluded from participating in classroom activities. Some bilingual pupils may also find themselves unable to respond to a teacher-initiated interaction because their communicative competence in English is not yet well developed unless, of course, it is either in the bilingual pupils' home language or with another bilingual pupil who is competent in both languages and translates or acts as a 'peer tutor'. This is a useful strategy for securing the language development of bilingual pupils, and communicating concepts and ideas to promote learning.

Research by Oglivy et al (1990) into staff attitudes and perceptions in multi-ethnic nursery schools confirms that staff adopted a controlling style of interaction with ethnic minority children as an overall strategy, disregarding individual pupil differences in ability. The quality and quantity of staff-child interactions were minimal. An earlier study by Ingham (1982) had also confirmed that adult-child contact in day nurseries were unexpectedly low. Gender and ethnicity were found to be influential factors in determining the quality and quantity of adult-child interactions.

The evidence from the preceding studies would suggest that bilingual pupils' language development could be at a disadvantage as a result of teacher neglect. Yet teachers tend to blame bilingual pupils' lack of progress on language problems . Oglivy's study revealed that staff had a laissez-faire attitude towards bilingual pupils' English language development.

... Asian children who speak little English are soaking it in and are just 'not at the stage' of speaking yet. Such misapprehensions regarding the nature of second language development, when combined with the directive not to tell Asian children to speak English, contribute to a language policy which consists of 'letting well alone' (Oglivy et al 1990:11).

Wright (1992) in her study and classroom observations, unearthed subtle differences in the manner in which white teachers in multi-racial primary schools treated black ethnic minority children. Wright observed that when nursery children came together as a group for story time and English language activities, where the teacher encouraged the children through discussion, talking about objects, stories and so on as a way of extending their speaking and listening skills in English, the South Asian pupils were generally excluded. The white teachers assumed that the South Asian pupils could not understand or speak English. When the teachers encouraged the South Asian pupils to participate in classroom activities, the requests to the children were often made in basic telegraphic language. If this failed, the teachers would quickly lose patience with the South Asian children and ignore them. When it was suggested to one of the teachers to encourage the South Asian pupils to use their home language the response was as follows:

But no, I don't encourage that (bilingual pupils using their home language), at least not in the normal classroom situation (Wright 1992:11).

Bilingual pupils were generally perceived as having learning problems emanating from language difficulties. Teachers disapproved of the use of the home language by bilingual pupils in their classrooms. Those bilingual pupils who turned to peer support from fellow bilinguals were seen to be acting as an exclusive group causing classroom management problems . However, approval was shown to those South Asian pupils who were perceived to be socially adjusted and integrated in the classroom and proficient in the English language. These pupils measured up to the teachers' ideal pupil construct, or according to Tizard et al (1988) these pupils were considered a pleasure to teach.

Tizard et al (1988) cited evidence to illustrate that there were significant differences in the school experiences of Black British African-Caribbean boys and girls compared to their white peers because the black children were often at the receiving end of racial taunts. In the Wright (1992) study, South Asian pupils' interactions with their white peers were also influenced by teacher attitudes. These pupils were extremely unpopular among their white peers who would refer to South Asian pupils by using the very same or similar derogatory terms used by their white teachers. It was almost as if the teacher had given such negative attitudes towards the South Asian pupils a seal of approval. If these pupils were being taught by a teacher who was sensitive to the children's language and culture, it was highly unlikely that the pupils would be at the receiving end of racial abuse. Even if they were verbally abused, it is probable they would have had better strategies to cope with the situation because as Milner (1983:168) suggests:

'The affection and respect that a good teacher engenders underwrites two important dimensions to the teacher-child relationship; one is the extent to which the child will take the teacher as a model and internalise the standards and values that she/he embodies; the other concerns the emotional and evaluative tenor of feedback from the teacher, which may *support* or *undermine* the child's feelings of self-worth' .

Conclusions

This chapter makes clear that bilingual pupils' early language development in school could be hindered because of linguistic and cultural dissonance between bilingual pupils and their white monolingual teachers. It was suggested that white monolingual teachers could find it difficult to secure continuity and progression in the development of bilingual pupils' language because the teachers may be unable to contribute to the pupils' Language Acquisition Support System (LASS). Bilingual pupils' language and culture cannot be viewed in isolation from the pupils' own identities and experiences. 'Treating all children the same' is therefore not a sound base from which to cater for the learning needs of all pupils because bilingual pupils' learning needs may be significantly different from those of the ethnic majority.

Collaborative group work can benefit pupils' academic and social learning (Wiles, 1981; ORACLE, 1980; Galton and Williamson, 1992) through peer-tutoring and support. The fear of failing or being ridiculed in public is largely removed for bilingual pupils during collaborative group activities.

The evidence so far suggests that teacher attitudes and expectations have a profound effect on pupils' learning potential and performance. Many white, monolingual teachers tend to have low expectations of ethnic minority pupils, they interact less with these pupils and hold racially negative attitudes towards them. The difference in languages and cultures between white teachers and bilingual pupils could have a negative effect on classroom interactions and overall learning progress of bilingual pupils. We advocate an increase in ethnic minority and bilingual teachers and more in-service education for monolingual teachers to learn and understand the cultural, linguistic and attitudinal factors which encourage or inhibit bilingual children's linguistic and cognitive development.

References

Alexander, R., Rose, J. and Woodhead, C. (1992) *Curriculum Organisation and Classroom Practice in Primary Schools*: A Discussion Paper, DES

Alton-Lee, A, Nuthall, G. (1993) Reframing Classroom Research: A lesson from the Private World of Children, *Harvard Educational Review* Vol.63 No. 1

Bellack, A. A. et al (1966) *The Language of the Classroom*, Teachers' College Press, New York

Bernstein, B. (1970) Education Cannot Compensate for Society, *New Society,* 26th February 1970

Biggs, A. P., Edwards, V. (1992) 'I treat them all the same' Teacher-pupil talk in multiethnic classrooms, *Language and Education*, Vol.5 No 3

Blair, M., Mayor, B. and Gill, D. (Eds) (1992*) Racism and Education: Structures and Strategies,* Open University/Sage

Blatchford, P., Burke, J., Farquhar, C., Plewis, I. and Tizard, B. (1985) 'Educational Achievement in the Infant School: the influence of ethnic origin, gender and home on entry skills', *Educational Research* Vol 27 No 1

Bornstein and Lamb (Eds.) (1984*) Developmental Psychology: An Advanced Textbook,* Lawrence Erlbaum, N.J.

Bourne, J. (1990) 'LEA provision for bilingual pupils: ESL, bilingual support and community languages teaching', *Educational Research* Vol 32 No 1

Bruner, J. (1985) *Child's Talk: Learning to Use Language*, Norton

Department of Education And Science (1988) *The Education Reform Act*, HMSO

Department of Education And Science (1989) *The Education Reform Act 1988: The School Curriculum and Assessment Circular 5/89*. HMSO. London

Dodson, C. J. (1985) 'Second Language Acquisition and Bilingual Development: a theoretical framework', *Multicultural Development* Vol 9 Nos 1 & 2

Donaldson, M. (1978) *Children's Minds*, Fontana Press

Edwards, J. (1985) *Language, Society and Identity*, Blackwell

Flanders, N. (1970*) Analysing Teaching Behaviour,* Adison Wesley, Reading Mass.

Foster, S. (1990) *The Communicative Competence of Young Children,* Longman

Galton, M., Williamson, J. (1992) *Groupwork in the Primary Classroom,* Routledge

Hammersley, M. (Ed.) (1986) *Controversies in Classroom Research*, Oxford University Press

Hitchcock, G. and Hughes, D. (1989) *Research and The Teacher,* Routledge

Ingham, E. (1982) 'British and West Indian Children in Day Nurseries: A Comparative Study', *New Community* 9 (1) pp. 423-430

Mercer, N. (1985) *Every Child's Language! Book 1*, Open University Press

Milner, D. (1983) *Children and Race: Ten years On*, Ward Lock Educational

National Curriculum Council (1993) *The National Curriculum at Key Stage 1 and 2*, NCC, York

Nias, J. et al (1989) *Staff Relationships in the Primary School*, Cassell

Oglivy, C. M., Boath, E. H., Cheyne, W. M., Jahoda, G. and Schaffer, R. H. (1990) 'Staff attitudes and perceptions in multicultural nursery schools', *Early Child Development and Care* Vol 64

Rist, R. C. (1970) 'Student Social Class and Teacher Expectations, Self-fulfilling Prophecy in Ghetto Education', *Harvard Educational Review*, 40,3 pp.411-451

Rogoff, B. and Mistry, J. (1984) 'Memory Development in Cultural Context', in *Developmental Psychology: An Advanced Textbook*, Bornstein, M. and Lamb, M. (Eds.) (1984), Lawrence Erlbaum, Hillsdale, N.J.

School Examination and Assessment Council (1993) *School Assessment Folder: Key Stage One*, SEAC, London

Shields, M. M. (1978) 'The Child as Psychologist: Constructing the Social World, pp.529 556, Institute of Education University of London

Sinclair, J. McH. and Coulthard, C. M. (1975) *Towards an Analysis of Discourse: The English used by Teachers and Pupils*, Oxford University Press, London

Siraj-Blatchford, I. (1990) 'A Positive role', *Child Education*, November 1990

Siraj-Blatchford, I. (1993) *'Race', Gender and the Education of Teachers*, Open University Press

Sleeter, C. and Grant, C. (1988) 'A Rationale for Integrating Race, Gender and Social Class' in Weiss, L. (Ed.) *Class, Race, Gender in American Education*, Albany, State University of New York Press

Tizard, B. et al (1988) *Young Children At School In The Inner City*, London, LEA

Vygotsky, L.S. (1986) 3rd Edition: *Thought and Language*, The MIT Press

Wells, G. (1978) 'Talking with children: the complementary roles of parents and teachers', *English in Education* Vol 12 No 2

Wells, G. (1986) *The Meaning Makers*, London, Hodder and Stoughton

Wood, D. (1988) *How Children Think and Learn*, Blackwell

Wright, C. (1992) 'Early Education: Multiracial Primary School Classrooms' in Gill, D. Mayor, B. and Blair, M. (Eds.) *Racism and Education: Structures and Strategies*, Open University Press

Chapter 9

Finding a voice:
bilingual classroom assistants
and their role in primary schools

Jean Mills

It is four-year-old Jagpal's first day at school. In common with several of
the other children he is bewildered and disconcerted by his surroundings,
and also probably by the English used by the staff and other children, since
he speaks Panjabi. When his mother leaves him he becomes distressed,
and although the teacher tries to comfort him he becomes increasingly
distraught, until Mrs. Sangha the classroom assistant arrives from a
neighbouring classroom and begins to console him, talking in Panjabi.
Soon he settles down and they play with the toy farm together. This short
scene, replicated many times across the country at the beginning of a term,
is only one illustration of how indispensable a bilingual classroom assistant can be. However, while their value is clear to those of us who have
worked with bilingual assistants, their roles and responsibilities are generally under-researched (Clark, 1987; Balshaw, 1991; HMI 1992). For
example, there is no section devoted to them in Bourne's (1989) research
survey of LEA second language provision, in spite of the fact that in many
schools the classroom assistant may be the only member of staff who
shares the language and culture of the local community.

Who, then, are bilingual classroom assistants? Where and how are they deployed? Generally, I will be discussing a group, most of whom are female, who support teachers in primary classrooms by carrying out ancillary tasks (usually with the youngest children), and who speak one or more of the major South Asian languages: Bengali, Gujerati, Panjabi, Urdu. However, even a limited survey shows us that we are not dealing with a homogeneous group in terms of employment opportunities and job title. For example, in many authorities bilingual assistants are most likely to be employed under Section 11 (a provision of the 1966 Local Government Act, which allows local authorities to claim from central government a proportion of the salaries of people working with certain ethnic groups. Most of these posts are in the education service. See Bourne, 1989 for a more extensive description).

A survey of five local education authorities in England revealed the following variations:

- **Authority A**, West Midlands. Assistants are deployed to individual teams but belong to one of four area teams. They attend in-service sessions either weekly or monthly, with the whole team or in a separate group, according to the arrangements in their area.

- **Authority B**, Yorkshire. The assistants' title is *Bilingual Support Worker* (in the neighbouring authority it is *Language Support Assistant*). There is an induction course; a *Pathways into Teacher Training* course, with support for GCSE English and Maths and weekly in-service meetings.

- **Authority C**, a London borough. There are no assistants employed under Section 11. Since bilingual children form ten per cent of the school population, speaking sixty to seventy languages between them, it is felt in the borough that this kind of bilingual support would be spread too thinly.

- **Authority D**, a London borough. A small number of assistants are employed who are literate in the majority languages and have the RSA Certificate in Community Languages. They attend weekly in-service meetings.

● **Authority E**, a London borough. No assistants are employed under Section 11 on the grounds that it would be bilingual provision on the cheap (and therefore without status), and that there is no career structure for these workers.

In each of these authorities, individual schools also employed their own assistants who might be bilingual but would not necessarily be covered by Section 11 in-service arrangements. It is also interesting to note the differences in title which suggest a difference in emphasis between the language support role and the ancillary role. The backgrounds and educational experiences of assistants are similarly varied and may range from language diplomas and certificates granted by the Royal Society of Arts, to the NNEB qualification (granted by the National Nursery Education Board, usually to those who intend to work in day nurseries), or overseas degrees and diplomas. Let us take, for example, three assistants with whom I am acquainted. Kulvinder, in her early twenties, was born in the UK and is of Sikh background and speaks Panjabi. She was educated at the local primary and secondary schools until sixteen when she went on to gain her NNEB certificate. She wants to develop her career and has taken further GCSEs and 'A' levels at evening classes, but is undecided whether to pursue nursing or teacher training. Tajinder, in her mid-thirties and also of Sikh background, speaks and is literate in Panjabi, and knows some Urdu and Swahili. She was born in East Africa and came to England in her early teens. She has a Bilingual Communicator's Certificate from the local FE college but feels that her interrupted schooling and young family hold her back from developing a career. She has run a voluntary Panjabi class after school but feels the need for training to cope with the wide ability range. Soraya, in her mid-thirties, is Muslim, was born in Pakistan, and trained there as a teacher. She speaks Urdu and Mirpuri Panjabi and is literate in Urdu and Arabic. When she married she moved with her husband to Libya and taught there for a time in a Pakistani school. She teaches Urdu and Arabic to her sons in the evening after school. She would like to develop her teaching career when they are older but would welcome help with her written and spoken English. It is clear that each of these assistants has different skills and qualities to offer their schools and also that their immediate and long-term training needs are quite different.

If we go on to look at how assistants work in classrooms we again discover intriguing similarities and differences. Firstly, of course, most bilingual assistants work as *classroom* assistants and therefore carry out all those duties that are appropriate to that role. As Balshaw (1991:8) points out with reference to special needs assistants, duties tend to fall into five broad categories: educational, pastoral, liaison, ancillary, physical. Ancillary tasks, such as photocopying, making tea, washing up, tidying and helping to maintain the classroom, form part of any assistant's role. But other aspects of their work always have the added dimension of their bilingualism. A survey of fifteen assistants in two authorities, and my own observations of others at work, reveal the use of bilingual skills in the following areas:

● **Educational**: curriculum support for reading, writing, science, maths; checking understanding of concepts; story reading and telling, singing songs and rhymes; audio-recording stories and songs; helping to identify children's special needs; helping with SATs; working with children who have special needs; assisting with physiotherapy and speech therapy.

● **Pastoral**: helping children to dress, with hygiene and first aid; comforting distressed children; supporting the social and behavioural routines of the classroom; helping children to play; giving prayers in assembly.

● **Liaison**: interpreting for teachers and parents as the situation demands; discussing with parents, teachers and psychologists children's statements of special needs; interpreting for social workers, dentists, doctors; talking to parents on induction days, parents' evenings and outside school; doing written translations or having them done by others; helping parents to fill in forms; accompanying parents on hospital visits; accompanying teachers on home visits; helping to organise festivals and parties.

Clearly, many of the educational and pastoral duties mirror those carried out by most classroom assistants, except that they have a bilingual dimension. What is interesting about this list is the range and extent of the translating and interpreting role. Many of these liaison aspects of the job are not within the normal experience of a classroom assistant and must place extra demands on bilingual assistants, of which, perhaps, their schools are not aware. Let us look in more detail at how assistants operate bilingually in the classroom. Time spent observing Tajinder (here referred to as Mrs. Virdi) revealed that, in common with other assistants, she continually made choices in her use of language, according to who she spoke to and the topic and purpose of what she had to say. Here is a typical morning in the Reception class:

9.10 a.m. Mrs. Virdi greets children as they arrive and chats to parents and children in English and Panjabi while collecting money and reading books. She turns to the class teacher, commenting 'Mommy's gone away somewhere, dad told me.' She fastens a child's hair, saying 'Tikka?' (*'OK?'*)

9.20 a.m. She takes two girls and a boy to the painting area, where they will make collage figures of themselves on card. As they work, Mrs. Virdi moves between English and Panjabi, interspersing instructions and teaching points, as these extracts indicate (words spoken in Panjabi are in italics):

M.V.   *What sort of things are there on a face?*

C.   Eyes

M.V.   *There's eyes. What else is there?*

C.   Nose.

M.V.   *There's a nose. Hanifa, what else is there?*

C.   Mouth.

M.V.   Mouth, well done. *Mouth isn't it?...* What colour's this?

C.   Black.

M.V.   Black. *What do you call this in Panjabi? Do you know what you call it in Panjabi? What do we call it?*

C.   *Black*

M.V.   *Black,* That's right. Okay now, can you draw me all the things you see on a face? You just say the thing...

C.   Mouth

M.V.   Mouth. Nicely, because this is for, we're going to put it on a card, so Deepa *make it* nice, nice, O.K.? *Make it nice?*

135

10.00 a.m. The collages are finished and tidied away and Mrs. Virdi sits with another four children who are writing their own stories in small booklets. Again she mixes her use of English and Panjabi as she scribes for them.

M.V.   *Do you see some more* shops?

C.   *Yes there were only a few things left.*

M.V.   *Oh were there only a few pages left?* Only a few things left in the shop (she scribes). *And did you come home then?*

C.   *Yeah then I came home and went out.*

M.V.   Um? *You went out? Sandip says* home. *Sandip came back home.*

C.   *Sandip came home*

M.V.   Sandip came back (scribes)... *And did you put everything in the* cupboard?

C.   *I put them in the...* cupboard.

M.V.   She put everything in the cupboard (scribes)

Throughout the morning different children approach to show their models and pictures. A boy arrives to have an apron put on and Mrs. Virdi chats to him in Panjabi. M.V. *Last week you weren't here. Were you not well?* (he shakes his head) *What was wrong? Tell me. What was hurting you?* (he whispers) *Was your stomach hurting? Was your mouth hurting? Were your legs hurting? Tell me.* (he mumbles)... *What was hurting?* Child: *Back.* M.V. *Was your back hurting? Aah it must still be hurting.*

After break the book writing continues as Mrs. Virdi helps Zubair: 'Fire by Zubair. What happens to your policeman?' Zubair: 'He's dead' Mrs. Virdi writes for him. 'The p-o-l-i-c-e-m-a-n wears a blue hat. Oy! Zubair. *Look, the policeman you know the thief? He goes into the shop, yeah? And then the policeman catches him.* The p-o-l-i-c-e- m-a-n catches the... He puts them in prison? H-e puts... *You look here I'm doing your work why are you looking over there?* He puts them in jail. *So that means you're right.* The po-lice-man g-oes home. O.K. take your pencil and can you write over my writing?'

11.45 a.m. It is almost dinner time. Mrs. Virdi organises the children in tidying up the classroom, chooses some to go to the toilet, and hands out badges to those who have meat, no meat, no beef. She supervises the dinner queue and the 'home children' on the carpet. As they wait, she and the class teacher discuss the children's work during that morning. Now Mrs. Virdi's own son arrives and she takes him home to lunch.

This apparently unremarkable session must be reproduced thousands of times in classrooms throughout the country. What are some of the choices that assistants like Tajinder constantly make and how do they come to make them? A constant choice for assistants, on both a conscious and unconscious level is when, where and with whom to use their languages. My observations suggest that this can be very personal and, while fulfilling a school's policy of promoting mother tongue use, can operate in ways unknown to monolingual teachers. For example, I observed two assistants who worked in adjacent classrooms with early years children. One assistant used Panjabi predominantly for reinforcing school routines, for social exchanges, and for comforting children. The other, next door, used Panjabi more in teaching exchanges to reinforce a point or to extend a point. In discussion with me both indicated that these were deliberate choices and that they used mother tongue in those situations to ensure more deliberate communication. Yet what a difference there would be for the children in the circumstances in which they heard their mother tongue in school. Tajinder, too, was very conscious that such decisions lay with her. As she said to me: 'On the ground I decide when and how to use Panjabi'. She also showed sociolinguistic sensitivity in matching language use to particular children and particular contexts. Thus she

● encouraged transfer of vocabulary items such as colours and parts of the body from English to Panjabi (and vice-versa) by embedding the word in a Panjabi phrase (Martin-Jones 1993:28 has very usefully categorised this as 'label-quest').

● Directed children's attention to the parallels in each language by such phrases as 'What do you call this in Panjabi?' The hidden message here for the children is that when two languages operate there are two labels for the same concept. Similarly, such comparisons imply that one way to learn is to consciously look for comparisons between languages.

● Made instructions and explanations more direct and explicit. It was interesting that the only direct reprimand of that morning was in Panjabi. As an example of the hidden curriculum of bilingualism, this occurred unknown to either the teacher or myself. One suspects that similar episodes are occurring in many other classrooms.

● Elicited more complex responses and provided parallel translations. In the book-making episode the response was often extended in Panjabi, rephrased in English into written standard form, and read out loud to the child as the letters appeared. In this way a very strong connection was made for the children between the English form and its symbolic representation.

● Used Panjabi for more intimate contexts, for example, inquiring about visits to the doctor. Very often choice of language is related to situation, and it is more natural, especially with young children, for Panjabi to be the favoured language for home and personal contexts and English for school, academic and formal contexts. Tajinder herself was well aware of sociolinguistic constraints when she pointed out to me the boy who came to have his apron put on and would not reply to her in Panjabi because I was present.

In these examples we can see the pattern described by Martin-Jones (1993:29) in which curriculum-oriented talk alternates with learner-oriented talk. That is to say the assistant is coping with demands that stem from her pastoral role as nurturer and her other role in ensuring access to the curriculum for bilingual children. Tajinder clearly sees that she has such a dual role. However, this might not always be the case, and in the example quoted above one assistant saw her role more as a nurturer. The demands on assistants are not, however, simply at classroom level in interacting with groups and individuals. As I indicated previously, because they may be the only people in school who speak a particular language, they carry out many other tasks particularly in terms of liaison with parents, the local community, and professional agencies. These bring with them other pressures which again are related to translation choices, but more especially related to the status and role of bilingual assistants. Thus bilingual assistants have related to me situations where they felt under pressure and inadequately prepared because they were being asked to operate in an unfamiliar register. One of these registers is the technical and semi-technical language of education. An assistant described an induction meeting for parents of new children where she was asked to translate for the head teacher who was explaining the workings of the National Curriculum. When she came to conveying such concepts as *National Curriculum, Programmes of Study* and *Attainment Target*, she fell back on terms like 'all the things we study in school'. Again, this same school held parents' meetings where different aspects of the curriculum were demonstrated by teachers. The assistant translating felt insecure in adequately conveying notions such as 'mathematical concepts' and 'the value of play in the Reception class', and felt at times that she was having to sell school policy to parents who, on the basis of their own educational experiences, were not at all convinced that their infant children should be playing with sand and water in school.

Similarly, certain nuances can be very difficult to capture exactly. Trying to persuade a mother to stay in school with her distressed child, an assistant wanted to explain that leaving him could be very traumatic. However, she could not satisfactorily translate this word and used a word for 'upset' instead, which she felt had not the power of the original, and was frustrated to find that the mother left the child to cry. Other assistants have described being asked to interpret in sensitive matters such as cases of suspected child abuse, or conveying to parents that their child had learning difficulties and that the school was recommending a place in a special school. In this latter case, the assistant felt that one difficulty was the Panjabi translation of the term 'special school' which sounded too severe. Later, a parent had berated the assistant as if she had been part of the decision making process, saying 'Are you telling me my child's mad?'. This final instance indicates that it is not just the language alone that can cause difficulties but also the nature of the role of interpreter that assistants sometimes unwittingly find themselves taking on. At parents' evening they may find themselves hearing complaints in Panjabi about a teacher as that teacher waits to be told what is being said. What is an appropriate professional stance in such a situation? It is not surprising that sometimes, as one assistant pointed out to me, they are apprehensive when they hear the phrase 'Come and translate', and that they learn to adjust their role accordingly. In the cases cited, this was by being neutral, 'staying between the school and the parent'.

The above indicates the need for support and training that is simply not related to the assistant's task of working bilingually with children in the classroom, important though this is. Such support needs to take account of those sociolinguistic constraints within which assistants operate and of which, as I have indicated, they are well aware. These include such areas as: professionalism. What elements would be part of a professional code for a classroom assistant acting in a liaison role? If assistants are called on to be interpreters they need to consider with their other colleagues an issue like confidentiality. This does not simply mean an understanding that certain matters should not be openly discussed outside the school. A school's management must also balance their immediate need for an interpreter against the pressure that assistants are put under in certain sensitive situations. Is it right that, for example, in the company of the educational psychologist and head teacher the bilingual classroom assistant may have to convey to parents quite upsetting information about their child, especially if they live in the local community and may be challenged about their role later? Many schools would use a bilingual teacher, if one were available, for such discussions. But the school may well want to raise the matter of the availability of professional interpreters with outside agencies like the psychological and social services. Moreover, even if the assistant isn't operating within a highly charged situation, part of the acknowledgement of her professionalism should be that there is time to establish with colleagues the purpose of particular interviews, possible cultural and linguistic difficulties, her role in resolving them, and there should be time for evaluation and feedback afterwards. This implies also that assistants should be included in a school's in-service arrangements so that they are more aware of some of the educational issues that they have to deal with and so that some of their special needs are catered for. Here there might well be a difficulty. Since assistants have a narrower job description and are paid less than teachers, how far can individual schools expect them to attend extra meetings or join working parties with colleagues? Heaslip's survey (in Clark, 1987:31) uncovered the resentment of nursery nurses if they were expected to develop their careers in what they considered to be their own time; the same response may well characterise bilingual classroom assistants. However, it would be helpful for all parties in interpreting exchanges, to be aware of particular rules that should be in operation. As interpreter, and not representative of the school, an assistant needs to avoid emotional involvement and be neutral between the wishes of parents and schools. If necessary, she needs the authorisation to withdraw from the interview. It is not for her to put pressure on either party but to convey as honest and exact a message as possible. This may mean having to obtain clarification or learning to intervene appropriately when misunderstandings arise.

As I have indicated, many of the classroom assistants I have worked with are linguistically very sensitive. This may not always be the case. Sometimes there needs to be an appreciation of appropriate formal and informal usage, tone, register, and the associations certain words have in different cultures (e.g. the pejorative associations the term 'Special School' had in Panjabi for the parents cited earlier). Thus, when I asked an assistant to help me assess a child suspected of having learning difficulties, I was surprised by her evaluation: 'She's barmy'. Again, this seems to be another area where prior discussion of possible pitfalls, and clarification of the intended message is needed. Classroom assistants carry out much of their job on other people's territory, and they are therefore used to having to establish relationships with several colleagues, exercising tact and sensitivity towards the feelings of others. Such skills are needed also in the liaison role, as are the ability to cope with the aggression or rudeness that may be focused on them as mediator, and the confidence to close down an interview if it has become unproductive. In short, assertiveness is an important characteristic. Moreover, qualities such as insight into the motives and attitudes of different parties in a discussion, and awareness of her own attitudes, are important to avoid the wrong message being received. Teachers, too, need to realise that this may happen and an impression they accept in good faith that a particular family is ignorant and uncaring about their children's education may be the result of a middle-class interpreter's attitude to social class, or a city dweller's perception of rural life. For example, some of the language varieties spoken by children in British schools have no written form and a lower status. Thus Urdu, a national and literary language, might well be preferred to Mirpuri Panjabi with its rural associations. It is very easy to judge others by one's own cultural norms, and also to accept uncritically information passed on by a representative of a particular community.

Conclusion

What have we learned, and how can bilingual classroom assistants be supported when they 'are invariably low-status staff... with few paths of professional development open to them' (Martin-Jones, 1993:26)? Because they are relatively scarce, and because 'asymmetrical social relations between monolingual teachers and bilingual assistants... (have) already been created by educational policy decisions' (ibid.), demands on bilingual classroom assistants are often high. Moreover, their experience is fragmented. They are a disparate group, having a range of languages, oracy and literacy skills, and educational backgrounds. In some authorities they are part of a team; in others they are employed by individual schools. This may mean there is no co-ordination of their in-service training or 'little understanding of the kind of linguistic or cultural contribution they can make to classroom practice' (ibid.). Unlike teachers, they may have little opportunity to meet colleagues and share common experiences. At the time of writing, there is great pressure on Section 11 funds, and on LEA services, agencies which, in the past, would have supported the career development of bilingual classroom assistants. Such people as Tajinder, Kulvinder and Soraya clearly enhance the education of children. The potential is there for training and development, but the responsibility tends to fall on individual schools, and fragmented agencies. A marvellous opportunity could so easily be missed.

References

Balshaw, M.H. (1991) *Help in the Classroom*. David Fulton

Bourne, J. (1989) *Moving Into the Mainstream. LEA Provision for Bilingual Pupils*. NFER-Nelson

Clark, M. (1987) *Roles, Responsibilities and Relationships in the Education of Young Children*. Educational Review Occasional Publications No. 13.

Clark, M. (1988) *Children Under Five: Educational Research and Evidence*. Gordon and Breach.

HMI (1992) *Non-teaching Staff in Schools*. HMSO

Martin-Jones, M. (in press) 'Code Switching in the Classroom: Two Decades of Research' in Milroy, L. and Muysken, P. (eds.) *One Speaker, Two Languages: cross-disciplinary perspectives on code-switching*. Cambridge: Cambridge University Press.

Chapter 10

Towards empowerment: training secondary school students as community interpreters

Jeanette Harman

'Speak loudly and slowly, then they'll understand'. Such was the advice given to me when I wanted to speak to the parents of Pakistani and Bangladeshi children as a new teacher in Birmingham in the 1970s. When this approach failed, both teacher and parent would leave feeling embarrassed and confused, with nothing achieved. Parents' evenings would be a nightmare of nervous tension, with conversation reduced to a few simplistic statements in English, much nodding and gesturing, and few questions asked by parents. The following was typical:

Teacher: Good evening — how are you?

Parent: Good evening.

Teacher: Shemeza is doing very well in class

Parent: Very well

Teacher: Is there anything you would like to ask me?

Parent: (nods)

Teacher: Shemeza does seem to be away from school rather a lot.

Parent: (looks puzzled)

Teacher: Are there any problems at home at all?

Parent: Thank you, good-bye

Teacher: Yes, good-bye

            (They shake hands, and the parent leaves)

It is no wonder that parents left as soon as they were able; nor that the majority of parents stayed at home rather than face such a fruitless ordeal.

Teachers and parents were frustrated by the futility of such a meeting. Recognising that they were not able to find out about their children's education in this way, communities employed a new strategy. Parents would now arrive at parents' evenings with an older child who could interpret for teacher and parent. Although this situation allowed dialogue about a child's progress, it would still prove unsatisfactory. Children were not always suitable interpreters of parent-teacher meetings. The use of children may be a short-term convenience, but in the long-term the message to the community is that schools and local authorities are not prepared to invest in their relationships with parents.

Later, schools employed bilingual community workers and classroom assistants who were able to interpret for the Pakistani (Mirpuri- speaking) and Bangladeshi (Sylheti-speaking) communities. Considerable demands were made on their time, while their professional needs were largely ignored (see Mills, 1994 in this volume). It is still rare for such workers to be offered training in interpreting skills. Schools largely make the assumption that because community workers or classroom assistants are (or appear to be) members of South Asian communities, they are necessarily experts in cultural and linguistic matters. In fact many bilingual staff choose to speak only English in school because the institution fails to provide an environment in which other languages have genuine status.

Community Languages in Aston, Birmingham

Many Pakistani families in Birmingham have origins in the Mirpur region of Pakistan. Their regional language has become known as Mirpuri. It has no written form; many Pakistani children go to their local mosque to learn literacy in Urdu, the state language of Pakistan. Most of the Bangladeshi families in Birmingham have roots in Sylhet, a rural area of NE Bangladesh. Their language has become known as Sylheti. Although there was once a written form of this language, it has largely been replaced as a language of business and education in Bangladesh by Bengali. Some Sylheti-speaking children in Birmingham learn Bengali at mosque or community school. In some Birmingham schools more than 90% of children are Pakistani or Bangladeshi. Many parents, particularly mothers, of Pakistani and Bangladeshi children in Birmingham speak only their home language. Smith (1976) reports that 77% of Pakistani women surveyed spoke English only slightly or not at all. Although this picture may have changed slightly since the 1970s, it is clear that schools still find it difficult to explain effectively to speakers of other languages the many changes in education of recent years. There is a continuing and pressing need for a properly trained, accessible interpreting service. Language, culture and class position should not prevent parents from understanding, contributing to and actively participating in their children's education (Delgado-Gaitan, 1990). Such involvement is only possible, however, when schools adopt planned strategies which reach out to disenfranchised parents who feel powerless.

The Need for Trained Interpreters

Trained interpreters can make a vast difference to the quality of interaction between school and community. There may exist a gulf between teachers and parents, not only linguistically, but also in terms of values and expectations of education. A sensitive, trained interpreter can begin to bring these attitudes together by explaining some of the cultural differences on both sides, and by steering professionals away from actions or words which may be insensitive or inappropriate. An untrained interpreter may be unable to put aside personal opinions and bias, and may therefore give a distorted interpretation of an issue to either professional or parent. One of the most important tasks for a community interpreter is to throw light on the differences in culture, values and expectations between the school and the community. Only an interpreter who is sensitive to such issues can perform this role usefully. Interpreters who are used on an ad hoc basis may be unsuitable for any of a number of reasons: they may be too young to discuss particular issues; they may come from an inappropriate social group in the community. The school may be ignorant of these factors, which are of immense importance in some South Asian cultures, and may have repercussions at interviews.

Some interpreting situations may deal with sensitive personal or family issues. Using a child family member is unacceptable. It could place undue strain on the parent-child relationship. Parents may feel humiliated by being placed in a dependent role. Children may be called upon to interpret material which parents would prefer the child not to hear. Rack (1982), writing in a different context, reminds us of the inappropriateness of using children as ad hoc interpreters:

Under no circumstances should children be asked to interpret medical details for their parents. It appears to us to be unethical, unprofessional, uncivilised and totally unacceptable.

In education we are too often prepared to make-do. Schools often assume that parents do not mind using their children as interpreters, but in fact they may mind intensely but feel it inappropriate to say so. When teachers need to discuss problems relating to children in their class, young sibling interpreters may be unable to interpret accurately. We should not make the mistake of assuming that because children are able to speak more than one language, they are always able to interpret easily. Children become 'cultural brokers' (Delgado-Gaitan and Trueba, 1991) as they attempt to interpret and negotiate between parent and teaching professional. Sibling interpreters may be put in compromising situations by teachers. It is not always appropriate for a child to speak to a parent about matters which may be culturally sensitive. Child interpreters have been forced to resolve the dilemma for themselves in a matter of seconds: should they tell their teacher that what has been said may cause offence, or risk the wrath of the family? Often the safest path through is to find a compromise by failing to interpret quite accurately for either side. Thus once more the school fails to provide parents with access to information about their children's education.

Using bilingual classroom assistants, community workers and teachers as all-purpose interpreters as a matter of course puts unfair pressure on them. Although they may comply with constant requests for help from their monolingual colleagues, bilingual school staff may resent this additional workload. Such demands are almost always made on top of existing duties, and carry no status in the school's structure. This approach, while well-meaning, also downgrades the skills of interpreting, assuming that all bilingual workers are necessarily aware of the cultural and linguistic complexities of the role.

Schools either positively encourage and invite parents to become involved in their children's education, or give the message that they are not welcomed (Delgado-Gaitan, 1990). Mirpuri-speaking and Sylheti-speaking parents need school staff to reach out to them in their own language and to speak to them about their children's achievements in the classroom. Pakistani and Bangladeshi parents are genuinely willing to participate in their children's learning; unless the school informs them in their own language **how** they can participate, they will continue to feel that they are unable to do so. Just as entitlement to curriculum and educational opportunities must be extended to all children, so must these fundamental rights be extended to all parents. We must ensure that the linguistic and cultural difference of Pakistani and Bangladeshi parents does not bar them from access to teachers (Wolfendale, 1992).

Training the Students

Recognising that the onus is on schools to take the first steps in providing access to their children's schooling, a colleague and I (both primary school teachers) set out to explore the possibility of local secondary school students as interpreters. As monolingual English teachers we could not act alone, and the project would have been fruitless without the help of two community workers, Fareida Beg, who acted as Sylheti interpreter, and Shafaq Hussain, who interpreted for the Mirpuri students. Shafaq and Fareida taught us much and demonstrated endless patience and enthusiasm throughout.

Six training sessions were planned, to take place at the secondary school. A certificate would be given to successful students as proof of competence. Our first meeting with the sixteen students took place in the hall of the secondary school. The students were initially apprehensive; when the training session began in their home language many of them were reticent, and even embarrassed. For them English was not only the language of the school but also of the street and the playground. Their home languages had been downgraded by both professionals and peer groups. The first responsibility for Shafaq and Fareida was to provide positive role models for these students, and to restore to them pride in their mother tongue. Discussions continued in Sylheti and Mirpuri, and it soon emerged that issues of racism were important to these young people who had previously felt that their voice was not recognised or valued. Most of the group were born in Britain, while their parents had been born in Pakistan or Bangladesh. They expressed feelings of anger and confusion about their bicultural experience; the training sessions became an important forum for the students to express their views. Many of them had experienced direct racism themselves, and needed to share these experiences; they sought affirmation of their feelings. They also needed to talk about the indirect racism which pervades our institutions. Many issues arose in which they found themselves in direct conflict between home and school. Muslim girls had experienced particular problems such as tension between family commitments and the desire for a career. It became apparent that the students generally lacked self-esteem, and much time would have to be invested in developing their confidence before they could become competent interpreters. This became a priority for Shafaq and Fareida. In the context of the open forum, in which previously unspoken views were expressed in their home language, the students began to develop greater self-confidence.

It was essential for the students to display a degree of professionalism, and not to be overwhelmed by the interpreting situation. The students had a deferential, respectful attitude to teachers; they would have to develop an ability to be assertive when a teacher's question may cause offence to a parent. The students needed much reassurance that it would not be offensive to challenge a teacher's judgement. Role play enabled the students to practice this skill. It was important that the students learned to establish with teachers the ground rules for interpreting before each interview. Guidelines were set as follows:

- Students should agree with teachers a style of interpreting: would they interpret each word literally, or summarise the main points? Would the teacher address the parent directly, or speak to the interpreter?

- How would pauses be used? Teachers should speak in sufficiently short sections to allow the interpreter to remember each point.

- Should the interpreter clarify any points independently? How would this be indicated to the teacher?

- The interpreter should be told of any specialist knowledge required well before the interview takes place, and should be aware of the teacher's objectives for the interview.

- The interpreter should make the teacher aware of any potential cultural conflict between the expectations of the school and community.

- The interpreter should ensure that the teacher is aware of appropriate forms of address of the parents.

- The interpreter should check that the parent and teacher are both happy to talk through the interpreter.

The impartiality of the interpreter's role was emphasised. The students began to understand the complex and sensitive nature of their new role. Initially they found it difficult to put themselves in the position of power-sharing with adults; much role-playing of the interpreting situation developed their confidence. Each role-play group consisted of a 'teacher', a 'parent' an 'interpreter' and an observer who took notes. Performance was examined, roles were swopped, and a sense of professionalism began to develop. The confidentiality of the interpreter's role was constantly stressed in the training sessions. A variety of seating arrangements was tried, allowing for direct eye-contact between the professional, the interpreter and the client. The students tried different ways of introducing interviews, and learned that introductions can set the tone and atmosphere in which interviews are conducted. Students were also made aware that they had the right to refuse to conduct an interview if they were for any reason considered to be an inappropriate medium for the discussion. We also prepared the students for the possibility that once trained, they may be regarded by both school and community as experts in language and culture. Heavy demands may be made. Once again role-play provided strategies for the students to deal with such pressures.

The students saw their role as important in empowering the community. During one of the training sessions we asked the students to brainstorm their views of the interpreter's role. These were some of their responses:

Rifat: Encouraging both sides to talk to each other.

Kabir: Explaining cultural assumptions.

Ishfaq: Empowering people.

Shahida: Enabling people to understand each other's point of view.

Shazia: Combating racism.

Monjul: Enabling people to speak freely to each other.

Siela: Making sure both sides know what's going on.

Nurun: Making sure that people don't miss out just because they don't understand English.

One factor which we had not taken into account at the outset was the students' concern that they might not possess sufficient vocabulary in their home language to interpret adequately. We were aware that some specialist vocabulary was specific to schools, and would not easily translate into Sylheti or Mirpuri; we role-played means of explaining phrases like 'National Curriculum'. We introduced the students to some of the technical jargon of the primary school. We had not foreseen, though, that the students would possess comprehensive vocabulary in neither English nor the home language. Their first language had become neglected due to its low status in British society. Their lack of proficiency in the home language, allied to their low self-esteem, had contributed directly to a lack of proficiency in English. Rather than both languages developing alongside each other, L1 skills were gradually being replaced by L2. They were therefore developing a 'semilingualism' (Skutnabb-Kangas, 1984), or 'subtractive bilingualism' (Cummins, 1989). It was our hope that by raising the status of Mirpuri and Sylheti, and giving the students the opportunity to use their languages in an authentic context, they would enhance their skills in both English and the home language.

Our next task was to train the primary school teachers in the use of the young interpreters. We were aware that for the teachers this would be a new experience. We encouraged them to be as open with the interpreters as possible, as the responsibility for the smooth running of the interview lay with the teacher rather than the interpreter. We reminded the teachers to speak clearly, avoiding jargon as much as possible. Finally we asked them to take care that the interpreter's home language matched that of the parent. We invited the student interpreters to the primary school to meet the teachers informally and to get a feel for the place before their first parents' evening. This would be their first opportunity to put into practice their new skills. We discussed dress codes with the students, encouraging them to look smart and professional. Traditional dress was encouraged.

Arrangements were made to collect by car any of the interpreters whose parents requested this.

Into Practice

Parents' evening arrived at the primary school. We did not see much of the student interpreters during the evening as they dispersed to various classrooms. At the end of the evening we gathered together briefly to share experiences. The atmosphere was excited and positive. The interpreters had been kept busy by the teachers, and had all enjoyed the evening. They had grown considerably since that first meeting in the hall of their secondary school. In the next few days we held a de-briefing meeting with the primary school staff, and asked them to complete evaluation forms. All of the comments were positive. Teaching staff felt that for the first time they had been able to hold meaningful conversations with parents. They had learned much and had been able to gain insights into the backgrounds of their pupils. They had improved their relationships with the parents. We met the young interpreters the following week for evaluation of the project. Their comments were also positive:

Ishfaq: I learned a lot about my own language.

Shazia: I have learned to talk to other people who understand me in my own language, without being scared or nervous. I have learned new words in my own language which I never understood before.

Nurun: This course was good for me because before I came here I seemed to speak my own language with English words in it, but now I don't seem to do that.

Siela: I have gained confidence in talking to others. I can now express myself in appropriate terms. I feel that I have played a part in helping the community.

There are important implications of the students' responses. These young people enhanced their language skills, their confidence and their self-esteem through the meaningful and purposeful use of their home language. We must question why Pakistani and Bangladeshi children and young people are effectively prevented from using their home language by an educational system which encourages them to leave behind their most natural learning medium at the earliest possible stage. In England monolingualism is regarded as the norm (Savva, 1991). Official and unofficial attitudes hold that anything else is a learning difficulty which must be rectified. Schools will generally support other languages only as a means to overcome them, so that they can treat all children as monolingual. These young students had been subject to these attitudes and policies throughout their education. Small wonder that they were initially embarrassed, even ashamed to be heard using their home language outside their own home. If the home language had been a genuine and authentic medium of learning in the classroom throughout their schooling, they would have been confident that their linguistic resources were a positive asset.

Secondly, the need for trained interpreters in multilingual schools became very clear. The parents in this community, as in any other, will only become active participants in society when they have full access to information about their children's education. This can be achieved when schools are organised to enable communication with parents in their own language. Until institutions and government at local and national levels give value and status to the training of community interpreters, many parents will continue to be marginalised by the British education system. The empowerment of communities relies on parents being able to talk to teachers. The training and employment of interpreters is a small step on the road to empowerment.

References

Cummins, J. (1989) 'Language and Literacy Acquisition in Bilingual Contexts' in *Journal of Multicultural and Multilingual Development* 10, 3.

Delgado-Gaitan, C. (1990) *Literacy for Empowerment.* Falmer, Lewes.

Delgado-Gaitan, C. and Trueba, H. (1991) *Crossing Cultural Borders. Education for Immigrant Families in America.* Falmer, Lewes.

Rack, P. (1982) *Race, Culture and Mental Disorders*, London, Tavistock.

Savva, H. (1991) 'Bilingual by Rights' *Language and Learning* 5.

Skutnabb-Kangas, T. (1984) *Bilingualism or Not: Education of Minorities* Multilingual Matters, Clevedon.

Smith, D. (1976) *The Facts of Racial Disadvantage*, PEP.

Wolfendale, S. (1992) *Empowering Parents and Teachers: Working for Children.* Cassell, London.

Chapter 11

'The flavour of the moment'? bilingual teachers' experiences of teaching and learning

Audrey Osler

This chapter examines the work experiences of bilingual teachers in the UK, noting the disadvantages and discrimination which many have encountered, and the impact of market ideologies on their careers. It focuses particularly on teachers' understandings and perceptions of their own schooling as bilingual learners and the influence these have had on their practice as teachers. Many schools serving multi-ethnic communities are in the process of reviewing their policies and practices to meet the learning needs of their students, and this can have a significant effect on the demands and expectations placed on bilingual teachers. This raises a number of ethical and political questions which schools need to consider in the employment of such teachers. The chapter will draw on data collected from recorded life history interviews with 48 black[1] teachers and student teachers, the majority of whom identified themselves as bilingual.

The employment patterns of black and bilingual teachers

The Swann Report (DES, 1985) devoted a full chapter to teacher education and the employment of ethnic minority teachers, noting the under-representation of ethnic minorities in the teaching force and the absence of statistical data. It included information from black teachers' organisations which suggested that ethnic minority teachers faced discrimination both in obtaining posts and in subsequent career advancement, frequently being obliged to accept temporary or 'supply' posts. The Committee's school visits highlighted a number of ethnic minority teachers who were 'stagnating' in posts which did not match their capabilities or experience (DES, 1985: 602).

Arguing that the teaching profession should reflect the ethnic make-up of the wider population and that black people should have access to professional positions, the Swann Report pointed out the potential of black teachers as a source of cultural expertise and as a reassuring point of contact for ethnic minority parents and children. The report stressed that it should not be assumed that black teachers will automatically fill such a role but that schools nevertheless had, in black teachers, a potential source of bilingual staff, teachers who might make a particular contribution to schools' pastoral programmes and develop community links. The report also stressed the value of ethnic minority teachers as role models to both black and white children.

The proportion of black teachers employed in the UK remains low. A survey undertaken on behalf of the Commission for Racial Equality (CRE, 1988) found that ethnic minorities were under- represented in the teaching profession, accounting for only 2 per cent of the teaching force compared with 4.5 per cent of the overall population. Black teachers tended to be on the lowest pay scales and to be disadvantaged in terms of promotion in relation to their white colleagues. The results of the survey provide useful statistical data which confirms the indications of the Swann report and of small scale studies by black teachers' groups (for example, Gibbes, 1980; Newham Afro-Caribbean Teachers' Association, 1985; Newham Asian Teachers' Association, 1985) that black teachers do not enjoy the same career progression or support as their white colleagues, with about half believing they have experienced racial discrimination in their employment. All the evidence suggests that black teachers are seen as a cheap commodity by their employers, more likely to be employed at lower pay levels and to be on temporary contracts.

A number of black and bilingual teachers have taken up posts funded under Section 11[2]. Section 11 funds have always been used to support the teaching of English and in the 1980s a number of local education authorities (LEAs) also introduced a range of curriculum initiatives in intercultural and anti-racist education under this source of funding, giving some participating teachers the opportunity for valuable professional development. Nevertheless, Section 11 funded posts have generally been viewed as low status; Newham Asian Teachers' Association (1985) reported that about one third of the borough's Asian teachers were employed under Section 11 and that there was a tendency for these teachers 'to be marginalised and not seen as an integral part of the school'. Recent changes in the administrative rules leave such teachers with low job security as contracts are issued for a fixed term in line with specific fixed term projects. As a consequence of employment patterns a disproportionate number of black and bilingual teachers are likely to be affected by these changes.

Bilingualism in the educational 'marketplace'

During the late 1970s and 1980s many LEAs took steps to implement equal opportunities policies in the recruitment and selection of teachers. Even in LEAs which introduced equal opportunities statements there was no guarantee that this would have a direct impact on the employment prospects of black teachers. In Newham for example, where the LEA had issued an anti-racist policy declaring its commitment to achieving equality in education and employment, the Asian Teachers' Association argued that the policy statement without effective action amounted to no more than tokenism (Newham Asian Teachers' Association, 1985). The vast majority of teachers had actively sought promotion, yet although a substantial number were shortlisted, over half reported that they had received no promotion at all since starting teaching; moreover, there was a relatively widespread perception that they were not given the same encouragement as their white counterparts, and were failing in attempts to achieve internal promotion within their schools. One disturbing feature of the survey was that all who participated reported at least occasional racist remarks from colleagues within the staff room.

The 1988 Education Reform Act and the introduction of local financial management has increased the autonomy of schools and significantly changed the nature of their relationship with LEAs. Although LEAs remain the legal employers of teachers in local authority schools, LEA advisers and inspectors have far less influence in those schools, and teachers who continue to work in schools which change their status to become grant maintained, effectively end their contracts with the LEA. In this context black and bilingual teachers are likely to experience greater isolation and be particularly vulnerable. The power of school governors has been increased and governors are likely to be far more influential in the selection and recruitment process. Research indicates that governing bodies are unlikely to be representative, being biased in favour of white, middle class males, who tend not to prioritise issues of equality and social justice (Deem et al., 1992).

This research would appear to support concerns expressed by the National Union of Teachers, in a policy document containing recommendations on 'the best means by which we can recruit, retain, motivate, involve and protect black teachers' presented to the 1990 Annual Conference, which noted that:

> possibilities for discrimination will be even greater if local authority guidance on equal opportunities practice is not heeded. Governors should be made aware that they may be financially liable for Industrial Tribunal cases if they do not take LEA advice and breach the Race Relations Act. The many black teachers who work in support services will also be made more vulnerable under LMS, as LEAs seek to reduce centrally held budgets in order to devolve finance to schools (NUT, 1990).

The rhetoric of the New Right emphasises parental empowerment and local accountability in the processes of schooling. Schools are seen as competitive units within a free market system and parents are viewed as consumers who through 'open enrolment', are invited to 'shop around' for a school which best meets their needs. The publication of schools' examination results and levels of truancy in the form of league tables is said to put pressure on schools to improve standards and to provide parents with valuable information which can form the basis of their 'choice'. It might be argued that such a system should favour bilingual learners, as schools will be obliged to consider their needs to ensure the maximum attainment of all pupils and secure strong places in the league tables. If it is accepted that bilingual teachers have particular skills which support the learning of bilingual children then they might also be expected to gain some advantage within the educational 'marketplace'.

The available evidence indicates the fallacious nature of such arguments. Popular and over-subscribed schools are able to introduce selection criteria which may discriminate against black and bilingual pupils. A recent CRE investigation into the schools' admissions policies of one LEA found that selection procedures at two over-subscribed schools were working to the disadvantage of those Asian parents who were unfamiliar with the British system of education and who themselves had some difficulties with the English language (CRE, 1992). Aspects of the schools' admissions policies were judged to be unlawful and to constitute 'indirect discrimination' under the terms of the 1976 Race Relations Act; the LEA and the schools concerned have since amended their policies.

Other cases which demonstrate that the principle of parental 'choice' may work selectively and against the interests of black and bilingual pupils are those of Dewsbury and, more recently, St Philip's Catholic sixth form college in Birmingham. In Dewsbury a group of white parents moved their children from a school where the majority of pupils were of South Asian descent. The foundation governors of St Philip's, a mixed sixth form college which includes large numbers of Hindus, Muslims and Sikhs, favour a return to a traditional Catholic boys' secondary school, against the wishes of the majority of the parents and students. They argue that they cannot provide a religious education in keeping with their constitution for the students, only one third of whom are Catholic (Mac an Ghaill, 1993).

Both cases are indicative of a dangerous ideology of cultural homogeneity, where greater emphasis is placed on the cultural and 'racial' differences between groups (ignoring cultural differences within groups) than on common humanity and shared human rights and values. Such notions of cultural homogeneity and of the 'naturalness' of racial difference as a basis for selection are likely to exclude black and bilingual pupils and teachers and to work against their interests in a free market system.

It is questionable whether bilingualism is necessarily seen as a marketable skill in England where monolingualism is perceived as the norm and where a colonial heritage leaves many monolingual English speakers with a sense of linguistic superiority. Karen Risager, writing from a Danish perspective, reminds us that the teaching of English should include some debate on the legitimacy of characterising English as a world language (1989), yet this debate is perhaps least likely to take place in England. Within the UK South Asian languages are often accorded lower status than European languages, as noted by this bilingual student:

> When girls speak their own language, the English girls look down on them. I don't think that's right because we should be able to speak whatever language we want. When the French come on exchanges and speak their language they're not looked down upon (Rasheeda, quoted in Osler, 1989: 13).

In such a context it would not be surprising if the skills of South Asian bilingual teachers are undervalued. Teachers responsible for Indian music and for the teaching of Urdu at Burnage High School reported how the school organisation served to diminish their status and that of their subjects in the eyes of pupils and staff (Macdonald et al., 1989). Most bilingual student teachers in this study with experience of teaching community languages in supplementary schools did not include this in their records of achievement, judging it to be of little interest to their university tutors.

The impact of bilingual teachers' own schooling

This data on bilingual teachers' experiences of teaching and learning is drawn from life history interviews with 48 black and bilingual teachers and student teachers living and working in the West Midlands and in London. The interviews took place over a period of some 20 months from the end of 1991 to mid-1993. Just over three quarters of the teachers and student teachers in the study were schooled, partially or wholly, in the UK. The group represented teachers who had been at school from the 1950s through to the 1980s. The vast majority of experienced teachers had begun their teaching careers in the 1980s, although some had worked in British schools during the 1960s and 1970s and a tiny handful had some brief experience of teaching overseas. The group had thus experienced, as teachers and learners, a significant shift in policies and attitudes towards the education of black and bilingual learners over several decades.

Black and bilingual children have long been perceived as a 'problem' in British schools, and the educational response to this perception can be traced through various policy approaches since the 1960s. It has been suggested at various times during this period that black students' language structures or skills are inadequate for successful learning, that they suffer from culture shock, inter-generational family conflicts, repressive or inadequate parenting, and identity crises. The problem has been seen to lie within the students themselves, in their numbers in schools, in their supposed family or cultural characteristics, and in their responses to schooling. Until the 1980s there was a reluctance to explore the question of whether the problem might exist within the education system rather than within black culture.

Tomlinson (1983) provides a useful review of the literature on policy, achievement, home backgrounds and black pupils over much of this period. Language was a key issue in assimilationist theory from the 1960s. The purpose of learning English was not just to improve communication, since as Troyna and Williams note, learning English was seen as 'the key to cultural and social assimilation and the means by which black students could overcome the 'inadequacies" of (their) language' (1986). It is worth noting that very different approaches were adopted towards children of African Caribbean and South Asian descent. Generally speaking, Asian children were identified as speakers of other languages and as being in need of English language support, originally in special centres or classes and, more recently, within mainstream schooling. African Caribbean children, by contrast, were not generally acknowledged as bilingual or bi-dialectical and consequently were characterised as speaking an inadequate or deficient form of English. Little direct language support was offered; a major concern within the African Caribbean community has been the disproportionate placement of children in schools for the educationally sub-normal and in disruptive units, and the more frequent suspension of African Caribbean children from mainstream schools.

The teachers in this study stressed the encouragement and support for education offered by their families, often contrasting this with what was seen as indifference, or in some cases discouragement, at school:

> My parents were brilliant about it, everything I learnt the old man taught me. He taught the alphabet and I knew how to count to 100 before I actually went to school, he taught me that. And when I got my first reading book I remember he had just come back from work and he called me downstairs and he started me straight away (Avtar).

> I did my O level maths and all along these teachers knew that I wanted to teach and they kept putting me off. *What do you want to teach for? Why don't you go into nursing? Why don't you be a social worker?* I went up to get my results and I passed eight O levels and the careers officer was there and he saw my results and he said, 'What do you want to teach for? Do welfare work or social work, what do you want to be a teacher for?' So I just ignored them basically, and my parents supported me all of the way. I had relatives as well who kept supporting me, continually writing letters from abroad encouraging me to get on with my work and do your best, get out of life what you want (Hazel).

The teachers reported the effects of negative attitudes towards their home languages on their own feelings about their bilingualism and on language learning:

> My mother said I wasn't all that fluent in Panjabi and as soon as I went to school I dropped mother tongue altogether and I wouldn't speak to her in mother tongue for a long time. And I have seen this now with other children. But at the time my mother was really worried about me. *Why has she suddenly stopped this and gone into English?* But I so wanted to belong, and I think all children want to belong.

> In fact I will be honest with you, I don't very easily now even, with the children in my class, drop into Panjabi, although I really want to and I try really hard. I didn't even value bilingualism, tri-lingualism, because I was taught to read and write Urdu. I used to go to a (supplementary) school where we would have Arabic and Urdu lessons. For about three years I went to these schools and it just didn't click in my mind that that was something to value, because nobody

else valued it. My mum and dad just felt it was their duty to make sure we had a bit of everything, but we were in Britain and so this was the language that we would have to be good in if we wanted to make anything of ourselves, so there was a bit of that as well (Salma).

Teachers emphasised, however, that parents were generally now much more determined that their children should be fluent in a community language, and comfortable with the idea they would use it alongside English in school; there was far more emphasis within families on preserving the child's home culture, language and identity than had previously been the case. Bilingual teachers were aware of the importance to parents of supplementary schools which allowed children to learn more of their community languages and culture, and critical of those colleagues who criticised parents for sending children to these classes.

Bilingual and bi-dialectical teachers were anxious that children should value their home languages and not suffer the same indignities and confusions that they themselves had endured; more particularly they were concerned that bilingual children should not be disadvantaged in assessment:

The only time that I felt embarrassment was when I'd say things that my mum would say to me. I'd repeat what my mum had said to the teacher and she didn't understand what I was saying and I didn't understand what she was saying— things that we'd call in West Indian terms were totally formed in a different way to white people, and I didn't know that at the time (Claudette).

I remember feeling as if we were dismissed more often than the others. We didn't speak English very well and there was this school trip and we were told that they needed the money but we weren't told when for. So I actually sneaked out at playtime and went home and got the money, and I found the gates locked when I got back. When I got back I handed in my money and she said 'I don't want it yet' and she was very rude (Ferdous).

In primary school I remember an assessment test that we had. They showed us some pictures and they said, 'What is this girl doing in the picture?' to all of us. This girl was having a wash, but this boy kept saying, 'She is tidying,' which is Creole for having a wash, and the teacher kept saying, 'What do you mean by that?' (Hazel)

Only a small proportion of the teachers had had black or bilingual teachers themselves and these particularly noted the difference this had made at primary school. When the first black teacher was encountered at secondary level there was sometimes a feeling of embarrassment, or a need to test this individual to establish whether they perceived themselves as sharing a common identity with other black people. More teachers reported being happier in primary than in secondary school. Although some felt this might have been because as small children they were unaware of the more subtle forms of discriminatory behaviour, a number believed their primary schools had shown a greater commitment to cultural and linguistic diversity. Bhupinder, for example, described her primary school where she felt the presence of Asian teachers and where the opportunity to speak with them in Panjabi 'made a very big difference'. This avoided a feeling of 'us and them' between home and school. She compared it with a secondary school where she felt the majority of teachers had colluded with racist and sexist harassment of students:

> White students started calling an Asian student 'Buddha' all of the time. The teacher wrote this name up on the blackboard and then himself would address the student as Buddha as well. This went on for some time until the student started staying away from school and what have you, until his parents came in (Bhupinder).

Most teachers stressed a special commitment to the needs of their black and bilingual students and some qualified this by explaining that, as a result of the experiences they had had, they felt a special commitment to any 'disadvantaged' pupil. Others reported that their own experiences of school made them determined to be sympathetic to the needs of every child in their care. It was sometimes a recollection of an unhappy or inadequate education which was the primary motivating factor in entering teaching; many of the student teachers in particular were confident that they would be able to make changes for the better.

In considering the contribution of black and bilingual teachers as role models for black children, some teachers felt that this role had become more critical since children now had a stronger sense of cultural identity. Children's experiences were different from those of their teachers, who had been subject to assimilationist policies, often in predominantly white schools. Today's children needed to know that black people had gone through the British education system and succeeded. Nevertheless, role models might be counterproductive if black and bilingual teachers were unable to progress.

Schools' needs

Schools are increasingly aware of the need for effective communication with parents and often require translation and interpretation services. Many schools with developing bilingual learners also recognise the need for specialist language support in the classroom. Limited budgets cause schools to consider the most effective use of existing resources. Often in such circumstances unreasonable demands are made on bilingual teachers and not enough thought is given to the ways in which monolingual teachers might extend their skills to become more effective teachers of all their pupils.

Shan (1990) notes how monolingual teachers often lack confidence in assessing bilingual learners. This would seem to extend beyond the processes of assessment and to be particularly acute in one-to-one communications with developing bilinguals. One African Caribbean science teacher described how he felt more comfortable working in situations where bilingualism was seen as normal rather than exceptional. At his school a large proportion of pupils spoke various South Asian languages, Greek and Turkish, and they were increasingly enrolling refugees. He reflected on the approaches his colleagues adopted towards these pupils:

> They rely on the in-class support that they get and some of them, I'm sorry to say, do tend to ignore those children that they can't communicate with. For instance, at the very end (of a lesson) they will say, 'Oh, Mehmet can you tell Arif what to do?' instead of showing the child and saying, 'Look I know you can't understand me but I'm going to tell you what to do and then get your friend to translate.' Some of them just can't be bothered to do that (Wesley).

This teacher had learnt Turkish and made a point of learning phrases in the various other languages used in school. As a black person he was particularly conscious of the damaging effects of racism on children, and felt that when working with newly arrived refugees it was particularly important to make them feel welcome and help them see that 'you're not racist against them'. While it might be idealistic to hope that substantial numbers of teachers will have the confidence and motivation to learn community languages there are clearly opportunities for monolingual teachers to adapt their practices to meet the needs of children with very limited understanding of English. It would also be an important step forward if more teachers, particularly foreign language teachers, took up Farzana Turner's challenge to learn 'one of the languages of Britain' (1989: 36).

There is often an expectation placed on bilingual teachers to take primary responsibility for communication with parents and community organisations:

> Everybody assumes that if you speak Panjabi or if you even look vaguely Asian you can read, write and translate in 10 different languages right away. I have to explain the difference in the spoken language, the written language, the fact that my education would be unusual if I was literate in Urdu and all this sort of thing. It has also been, not asked, but expected that I do more with parents. No one else would be asked to do lots of translation as soon as they have walked in the door. Even the other week I was told, 'We want to arrange a visit to the mosque'. I said 'Well, if it doesn't really fit in to what we are doing in terms of the classroom, I can help you with it but it is not the main thing I am going to be here to do, that is not what my job is'. Because I was Muslim and I was there they thought, *Oh well, she can do this* (Neelum).

Neelum's experiences and the assumptions made about her role and abilities based on her ethnicity, were not uncommon among the teachers in the sample. As a black woman, and as a Muslim, the school was ascribing to Neelum the role of 'professional ethnic' (Blair and Maylor, 1993). Yasmin, an experienced science teacher, was engaged on a supply contract in a school with a number of science vacancies. The head of science approached her and asked her if she would like a job teaching English as a second language. She had no expertise in this area:

> That really brought it home to me then. You only see a black woman, you don't see a science teacher. You see a woman and most E2L people are women. You see me as a black person who might be useful in this field, but who couldn't possibly have anything else to offer (Yasmin).

Surinder, a mathematics teacher in her first year, was one of a number who felt that schools should not exploit bilingual teachers, but be prepared to pay for translation and interpretation services:

> One of the head of houses came up to me and said, 'Do you speak a mother tongue? Could you translate something?' I did feel like saying, 'Well, you should pay someone to do it'. I said, 'I could give you some advice on it. I couldn't do it but I could find someone who could if you wanted me to'. I can't do a professional job of translating something in Panjabi (Surinder).

In the same way that many schools expect to use bilingual teachers' skills for additional professional duties, without any acknowledgement or reward, so too, many schools seek to exploit the skills of bilingual classroom assistants, making additional demands that are not expected of monolinguals. A number of schools may be in the position of employing bilingual classroom assistants who for various reasons may not have had access to higher education in the UK and hence to teaching qualifications. Some bilingual teachers whose qualifications were not recognised in this country have taken up positions as classroom assistants. Schools who deploy such assistants in similar ways to teaching staff may be using them as cheap labour. Bilingual classroom assistants may be seen as more 'flexible' than bilingual class teachers in primary schools since they can move from class to class and thus support many more bilingual learners. If bilingual classroom assistants are employed instead of bilingual teachers then, it may be argued, they are exploiting bilingual classroom assistants on low wages. At the same time they are undervaluing teachers' skills and viewing them as 'professional ethnics' rather than as teachers with a professional training.

Recent proposals to provide training for primary classroom assistants as 'Specialist Teacher Assistants' (TES, 1993) are likely to be widely welcomed. Nevertheless, further thought needs to be given to the support and development of classroom assistants and in particular to those bilingual classroom assistants (usually black women) who have the potential to train as teachers but who may have been disadvantaged in their own schooling.

The way forward

One teacher in this study suggested that black teachers should make the most of current career opportunities since they are 'the flavour of the moment'. Her comment reflects a degree of cynicism concerning employers' long-term commitment to black teachers. While some urban LEAs serving multi-ethnic communities have in recent years sought to increase their proportion of black and bilingual teachers there is no evidence that these teachers' careers have benefited from such commitments. Indeed, one LEA's recruitment drive aimed specifically to attract black and bilingual teachers appointed just three black teachers although 140 new teaching posts were created. Although the LEA had an equal opportunities policy, a number of ad hoc recruitment practices served to encourage personal patronage and work against the interests of black people. These included word of mouth recruitment; interviews at colleges not known to attract black students; the use of informal telephone references to exclude people from interview shortlists and an exclusively white recruitment team (Brar, 1991).

Black and bilingual teachers have benefited from support networks that they have set up. LEA support for such networks might assist in their development and encourage new teachers to become involved, so overcoming the isolation which many experience. Some young teachers expressed concern about open involvement in such groups, fearing that they would be perceived as 'having a chip on their shoulder', yet they also felt that networks might offer valuable support and encouragement. LEAs should provide information about networks to newly qualified teachers, recognising the service which they offer to their members. This might enhance the status of such groups among teachers generally. The valuable networking and support role provided by black advisers and advisory teachers to black and bilingual teachers in school also needs to be acknowledged. Young teachers in particular were encouraged by seeing black colleagues in high profile positions.

The support of senior management in schools is critical to black and bilingual teachers. Teachers often take on additional responsibilities in the hope that these will enhance their future career prospects, but black teachers have all too often found that these rewards do not come to them. One reason that bilingual teachers do not enjoy the same career progression as their white counterparts is that they are less frequently recognised as having the potential to fill senior posts:

> You do sense, as a black teacher, the lack of confidence among white teachers. I think it is stronger in senior management because they are the ones who actually hold the power, when it comes to interviewing or delegating duties. From the probationary stage, right through, you are not (seen to be) as competent as the white staff. You have to prove yourself on two levels, not just as a professional, as a teacher, but almost as a person, that you cannot only do their job, but that you can do it better than somebody else (Balbir).

Headteachers urgently need to tackle this issue and ensure that all members of their staff team have the opportunity to achieve and progress to their full capabilities.

Conclusion

Given the decreasing influence of LEAs and the increased autonomy of schools, the role of headteachers and senior management is critical in ensuring that black and bilingual teachers experience equality of opportunity to progress and develop professionally. Schools should identify and make public the criteria they require for promotion and for each individual post. Headteachers must go further than exploiting the 'cultural expertise' or language skills of black and bilingual teachers by appointing them to junior posts. Appropriate support will include the recognition of individuals as having particular professional strengths and capabilities, and a full staff development programme which encourages and supports the appointment of black and bilingual teachers at all levels.

Notes

1. The term 'black' is used here to describe people of African, African Caribbean and Asian descent within the specific political context of Britain; groups of people who share an experience of racism. It does not assume cultural homogeneity or homogeneity of experience.
2. Special funding arrangements made under Section 11 of the 1966 Local Government Act for the needs of ethnic minority children.

References

Blair, M and Maylor, U. (1993) 'Issues and Concerns for Black Women Teachers in Training' in I. Siraj-Blatchford (ed) *'Race', Gender and the Education of Teachers.* Buckingham: Open University Press.

Brar, H. S. (1991) 'Unequal Opportunities: the recruitment, selection and promotion prospects of black teachers'. *Evaluation and Research in Education,* 5, 1 & 2.

Commission for Racial Equality (1988) *Ethnic Minority School Teachers: a survey in eight local education authorities.* London: CRE.

Commission for Racial Equality (1992) *Secondary Schools Admission Report of a Formal Investigation into Hertfordshire County Council.* London: CRE.

Deem, R., Brehony, K., and Hemmings, S. (1992) 'Social Justice, Social Divisions and the Governing of Schools', in D. Gill, B. Mayor, and M. Blair, (eds) *Racism and Education.* London: Sage.

Department of Education and Science (1985) *Education for All: the Report of the Committee of Enquiry into the Education of Children from Ethnic Minority Groups.* The Swann Report, HMSO, Cmnd 9453.

Gibbes, N. (1980) *West Indian Teachers Speak Out their experiences in some of London's Schools.* London: Caribbean Teachers' Association and Lewisham Council for Community Relations.

Macdonald, I. et al. (1989) *Murder in the Playground: the report of the Macdonald Inquiry into racism and racial violence in Manchester schools* (The Burnage Report). London: Longsight.

Mac an Ghaill, M. (1993) God, the Enlightenment, Cultural Identities and St Philip's Sixth Form College: defence of comprehensive education. *Forum,* 33, 2.

National Union of Teachers (1990) *Memorandum of the Executive on Black Teachers: Annual Conference 1990.* London: National Union of Teachers.

Newham Afro-Caribbean Teachers Association (1985) *A Report on the Working Conditions and Status of African-Caribbean Teachers in Newham.* London: Newham Afro-Caribbean Teachers Association.

Newham Asian Teachers' Association (1985) *Racial Discrimination in Education.* London: Newham Asian Teachers' Association.

Osler, A. (1989) *Speaking Out: Black Girls in Britain.* London: Virago.

Risager, K (1989) 'World Studies and Foreign Language Teaching: a perspective from Denmark, *World Studies Journal,* 7, 2.

Shan, S-J. (1990) 'Assessment by Monolingual Teachers of Developing Bilinguals at Key Stage 1', *Multicultural Teaching,* 9, 1.

TES (1993) 'Mum's Army' demobbed. *Times Educational Supplement* 26 November.

Tomlinson, S. (1983) *Ethnic Minorities in British Schools.* London: Heinemann.

Troyna, B. and Williams, J. (1986) *Racism, Education and the State.* London: Croom Helm.

Turner, F. (1989) The Languages of Britain: 'What's wrong with Panjabi, Miss?'. *World Studies Journal,* 7,2.

Index

Child Migrant Education Program 84,
86, 87
Childe 102
Churchill 7
Clark 131, 140
Cleland 90
Cochran 79
code-mixing 53, 54
code-switching 53, 54
collaboration 121, 122
Commission for Racial Equality 154,
157
community 25, 106, 145
community workers 144, 147
Cook Island 22
Corson 1-15, 19, 20, 21, 23, 26, 28
Coulthard 118
Cox Report, The 61
cultural sensitivity 146
culture
— and identity 27,49, 57, 68
— majority 15, 102
— minority 15, 102, 118
Cummins 2, 7, 8, 11, 34, 46, 51, 54,
56, 150

Davison 83-99
Department of Education and Science
113
Deem 156
Delgado-Gaitan 71-74, 144-147
Denmark 158
Dewsbury 157
Diaz 71
discrimination 154, 157
diversity 51, 84
Dodson 50,114
Donaldson 120
Dorsey-Gaines 72

Education Reform Act 113, 156
Edwards 116, 119, 125
empowerment 59, 103, 143
English as a Second Language 11,
83-99

ethnicity 121, 126
equal opportunities policy 155
Evans 90

family 62, 106
family literacy 71-81
Fasold 1, 13
Finnish 6, 10
Flanders 118
Foster 122
Freire 72, 74

Gallimore 71, 73
Galton 120, 122, 127
Garcia 5,14
Gibbes 154
Gibbons 91
Goldenberg 71,73
Grant 118,119
Green 71, 75
group work 120
Gujerati 132
Gumperz 73

Habermas 2
Hagman 6
Hale 73
Harley 10,11
Harman 143-152
Heath 72
Heaslip 140
Hindi 62,63
HMI 131
Hodson 24
Holmes 27
Horvath 4

immigration 73-103
Ingham 116, 119, 126
interactional codes 103
interactive education 106
interpreters 89, 134, 136, 139, 143-152
Iraqi 98
IRF 119

Japanese 11

Kay 91
Keatinge 6
Khmer 98
Knight 101-111
Koch 32

Lahdenpera 6
Lamb 125
Lambert 3
language
— interdependence 51
— interference 53
— policy 19-40
language acquisition 6
Language Acquisition Support System
116, 129
Language Alive! 62
Levine 46, 107
liaison 134
Lo Bianco 87
Local Management of Schools 156
London 132
LPAC 19

Mac an Ghaill 157
Macdonald 158
McLaughlin 9
Malay 44
mainstreaming 84, 88
Maori 10
Marland 19, 21, 22, 25
Martin 86, 87
Martin-Jones 137, 138, 142
May 19-40
Maybin 19, 26, 28
Maylor 164
Mehan 71
Mercer 116, 120, 121, 123
metalinguistic awareness 54
Mexico 73
Mills 131-142, 144
Milner 127
Mirpuri 44, 141, 144, 147

Mistry 123
Moll 72
monolingualism 150
Moorfield 5
MOTET 6
mother tongue
— as educational medium 1
— assessment 51
— maintenance 8, 11, 48
— story 44
motivation 121
multicultural education 15, 44, 84,
105, 108
Muysken 9,11,28

Nahuatl 73
National Curriculum 101, 113, 114,
139
National Curriculum Council 121
National Union of Teachers 156
New Right 156
New Zealand 10, 19-40
Newham Afro-Caribbean Teachers
Association 154
Newham Asian Teachers Assocation
154, 159
Nias 117
Niuean 22
Nixon 62
NNEB 133
Nuthall 114, 117
Nyakatawa 113-129

Oglivy 116, 119, 126
ORACLE 120, 127
Osler 153-168
Otheguy 5, 14

Panjabi 131, 132, 137, 138
Parents, evenings 143, 151
Piaget 121

Race Relations Act 156, 161
racism 68, 104, 125, 127,148, 155,
159, 162, 163, 167

171

Rack 146
reading 71
Reeves 61-70
refugees 163
Rehbein 9
Risager 158
Rist 124, 125
Rogoff 123, 124
role models 154, 162
Romaine 2, 8, 28, 53, 54

Samoan 22
Savva 45, 48, 51, 53, 57, 152
school governors 156
SEAC 122
Section 11 132, 142, 155
self-esteem 121, 148
semilingualism 150
Shan 51, 163
Shields 118, 123
Sign Supported English 67
Sikh 124, 133
Sinclair 118
Siraj-Blatchford 113-129
Skilbeck 20, 39
Skutnabb-Kangas 2, 8, 10, 12, 150
Sleeter 118
Smith 145
Smyth 26
Snow 72
Spanish 6, 72
Specialist Teacher Assistants 165
Standard Assessment tasks 114
Stenhouse 20
supplementary schools 154, 161
Swain 7,8,46, 51, 54
Swann Report, The 61, 158
Sweden 6,10
Sylheti 44, 68, 144, 147, 150
Szwerd 74
Swahili 133

Tansley 52
Taylor 72, 74
TESOL 87
Thompson 26, 27
Theatre-in-Education 61-70
Tizard 127
Tomlinson 159
Tongan 22
Toukamaa threshold hypothesis 7
transference 62
Troyna 159
Trueba 61, 71, 73, 146
Turner 164

UNESCO 1, 14
United States 6
Urdu 47, 132, 135, 141

Vasquez 71
Vietnamese 98
Voicebox 66-70
Vygotsky 54, 116, 121

Weade 75
Wells 119, 123
Welsh 122
West Midlands 132
Wiles 120, 127
Williams 159
Williamson 120, 121, 127
Wolfendale 147
Wood 115
Wright 116, 119, 126, 127

Yorkshire 132
Yu 11